Hero

Hero

Being the strong father your children need

Meg Meeker, M.D.

REGNERY
PUBLISHING
A Division of Salem Media Group

Regnery® is a registered trademark of Salem Communications Holding Corporation

Cataloging-in-Publication data on file with the Library of Congress

ISBN 978-1-62157-502-3

Published in the United States by
Regnery Publishing
A Division of Salem Media Group
300 New Jersey Ave NW
Washington, DC 20001
www.Regnery.com

Manufactured in the United States of America

10 9 8 7 6 5 4 3 2

Books are available in quantity for promotional or premium use. For information on discounts and terms, please visit our website: www. Regnery.com.

Distributed to the trade by
Perseus Distribution
www.perseusdistribution.com

This book is dedicated to the great fathers who have personally inspired me to champion your outstanding examples.

My husband Walt.

To my brothers Mike and Bob Jones and my brothers-in-law Dan White, Ben McCallister, and John Linfoot.

To the younger fathers: Alden, Brandon, Michael, Freddy, Brad, Luke, Bo, Cory, and Josh.

And for those who will be dads: T and Jonathan. May you always look at the tremendous role models you have had and follow their leads.

And most importantly to the great men who came before us all: My father, Wally, and my father-in-law, Bo. Thank you for leaving your strong imprint on all of these men.

CONTENTS

Foreword

Dave Ramsey

More than a decade ago, I started reading Dr. Meg Meeker's books on parenting and walked away impressed with her wisdom and insight. Even more, I appreciated her passion for helping moms and dads navigate every twist and turn on the path to raising healthy kids.

Later, I got to know her personally and saw her heart for parents firsthand. It didn't take long for us to become close friends because we really were kindred spirits.

Back then, my children were in their late teens and early twenties. Now, as I sit down to write the foreword for this fabulous book, things have changed in the Ramsey family. These days, my kids are all grown, and I'm known as "Pappa Dave." I watch with pride as my sons-in-law throw my grandchildren into the air and make those toddlers squeal with delight. It helps me see the importance of dads through a new set of eyes.

It's funny, but I've never really seen their mothers play that game. Maybe it makes them too nervous, but I honestly think it's something that just fits the role of dads. It's a special task reserved for them—an activity they're uniquely qualified to perform.

Looking through the eyes of Pappa Dave, I can clearly see the different roles mothers and fathers play in the development of a healthy, confident child. Moms provide an absolutely essential function in the process. But so do dads—and that's something we should never forget.

Unfortunately, I'm afraid too many folks *are* forgetting it today.

Dr. Meg often points out that this generation of fathers has become the butt of all kinds of jokes, especially in the media. In television shows, commercials, and movies, you rarely see strong fathers portrayed. When you stop and think about it, it's tough to find *anything* in the world of entertainment that shows fathers in a positive light.

We can blame that on Hollywood or bad comedy or misguided parody. But whatever the source of the trouble, we have to admit that the problem is real.

Too many males in our culture have been "wussified" by the winds of political ideology that have blown across our country. As a result, they've lost their seat in their own households. So, while they are physically present, they are not spiritually or emotionally present.

Dr. Meg is absolutely right: Men—especially fathers—are in desperate need of rebranding.

When I look at my sons-in-law with my grandbabies, I can't help but think about how important it is for someone to tell them just how *valuable* they are. Someone needs to remind these young men—and millions like them—that they are neither court jesters nor ogres. Someone needs to come alongside them and teach them how they can be great fathers—the kind of fathers that firmly, gently, and lovingly lead their families.

Someone needs to tell them how much they *matter* in the development of their children.

Otherwise, kids will inevitably grow up with a dad-shaped gap in their lives. Dads teach risk, while also providing the security of firm boundaries. Dads see the jerk boyfriends coming from a mile away—and keep them away from their teenage daughters. And let's be honest... "fun" with dads is a completely different animal than the fun kids have with moms.

Not better. Just different.

And when culture fails to support fathers—when no one esteems them or teaches them how to be great—we do our society a disservice. We've got to help fathers become the men God has called them to be.

I believe Dr. Meg has the antidote for this crisis of culture. God has anointed her in a special way to address this topic. He has raised her up to stand in the gap and to offer hope for such a time as this.

But it's only fair to warn you... by the time you finish this book, you'll be ready to buy cases of them. You'll want to give them away to as many fathers as you can. It will become your go-to gift every time you come across a dad with a new baby. And it won't just be because this is a great book; it's because you'll become convinced just how desperately the world needs this message.

It's time for the men in this country to rise up, stand firm, and truly become the heroes their kids need them to be. I truly believe that, with a world full of strong fathers, there's simply no limit to what the next generation can achieve.

CHAPTER 1

You Are a Hero

On March 30, 2011, I held my father's hands for the last time. These were the hands that taught me to cast a fly rod, shoot a 7 mm Mauser, and guide me across the streets of Boston when I was a little girl. Today, they were soft. They were once leathery from working outside feeding cattle or riding horses; his index fingers were stained from tamping tobacco into the mouth of his pipe.

Now they were soft and smooth because they belonged to a man who had suffered dementia for four years. He didn't need these hands in the same way, but still I loved holding them. They were my father's, *my* father's hands, and that's what made them dear to me. As I held his hands that day, I did what I had done for months and months. I read aloud to him from the books he had on his bookshelf. He couldn't speak any meaningful words and I wondered if he knew me. I wanted him to say my name but he couldn't. I wanted him to know that the hands that held his were mine. I think he did because when I sat with him, he became calmer. Sometimes he would cry a little bit when he heard my voice.

The last years of my father's life were painful for me but much worse for him. As dementia set in, he knew it. Many months during those in between years when he was mentally sharp but losing solid cognitive function, he cried a lot. I would find him sitting alone in the family room on the couch just crying. I knew the reason he cried but reassuring him that life was going to be all right was a challenge. It wasn't going to be all right for him. He was losing himself—his connection to anything meaningful in his life. And we were losing our connection to him, in a way. He was morphing into a man who would seem peculiar to us—gentler, more childlike. My father in the prime of his life was anything but childlike. He was a strong intellectual behind whose quiet demeanor was a fiery temper. He didn't need to speak much. We knew what he thought, what he wanted, and what he believed about us, his family. We knew that he would do anything he could to provide for us and protect us, but now he couldn't care for us as a father. And he knew it, and that killed him.

I remember the last Christmas that he *knew* was Christmas. He and I went to buy my mother a present in November. I wrapped it up and set it on the dining room table so that he could see it every day. But every day he asked again and again, "Have I bought mother a Christmas gift yet?" My answer was always the same, "Of course you have, Dad. You always do."

My dad was a brilliant physician turned cattle breeder—but that was just to make a living. Making sure that my mother, my two brothers, my sister and I were taken care of was always his first priority. He cared so much that we didn't want to let him down, and that made us better people. We wanted him to feel successful because he *was* successful, not only in his work, but more importantly as a dad.

This was no small feat for my father because he didn't have a great relationship with either of his parents. I'll just say it. His mother was mean. When my father was thirteen years old, he saved up money he made delivering newspapers and bought a pony. He kept it at his aunt's farm. One day he went to feed the pony and found that it was gone. His mother had sold it out from under him because she felt that he didn't need it anymore. No warning, no conversation about why the pony should be sold, she just sold it. My father was crushed and as we walked the halls of the nursing home he stayed in during his last days on earth, he still talked about that pony.

So being a compassionate and caring father was a learned skill for him. I don't think that he had any clue about how to be a good dad. He just learned as he went. It flowed out of him, because he, like every father reading this book, had all the hardwiring necessary to be a great dad; it's innate; it's part of your DNA; you just have to use it. Sure, my dad, as a father, made a lot of mistakes along the way, but his successes overshadowed them. He lost his temper but he said he was sorry. He lived with humility because he knew his inner demons. He missed many of my lacrosse matches but I didn't care because I knew *he still cared*. I knew he believed that I could be successful, go to medical school, and become a pediatrician. He was always eager to ask questions of me and my siblings. He wanted to know what we thought, believed, felt, did. Every summer he insisted that the entire family spend two weeks together hiking and fishing in remote northern Maine. Not exactly a teenage girl's dream vacation. Often we tried hard not to go along but in the end my siblings and I were grateful that we did. Those vacations underscored that we mattered to him—and that we mattered to each other.

On March 30, as I sat with my father during his approach toward heaven, I felt an intense discomfort. I was a grown woman with grown children. I had a life of my own and loves of my own. So where, I wondered did this anxiety come from? It wasn't simple grief over losing a loved one. It was a panic that something in the center of my life was about to collapse. It didn't make sense intellectually but it made perfect sense to me emotionally. And then I put my finger on it. My dad was my safety net. Or to put it another way, he was the hub in the center of our family wheel and when that was gone, what would happen to me?

My father, not my husband, was the one I always thought would make everything right. If my world was falling apart, my father was the one I counted on to step up and put it together again. Memories of his quiet strength flooded my mind and I began to cry. I remembered the fall of my freshman year at Vassar College when I was homesick. On Friday afternoons, my dad would drive four hours to pick me up so I could spend the weekend at home, returning me on Sundays. He never complained, he just drove. I remembered when I was stranded at the Denver airport. My dad came to the rescue. I knew he would. He and my mother were in Denver, too, and had the foresight to place a reservation at a nearby hotel when it looked likely that a snowstorm would cancel flights. I was stubborn, though, and went to the airport, hoping to fly home. But after many hours of waiting to be rebooked on a flight that wasn't cancelled, I called them.

My father had already booked a room for me. I didn't have to sleep on the airport floor.

I could always rely on dad—even when I thought, initially at least, that I didn't want to. When I had burdens or pressure he always took them on himself. If I was drowning in hot water, he always came to the rescue. That's what dads are to their kids, or what their kids want them to be—a hero they can always depend on. And one day, as they see you slip from their lives as I saw my father slipping from mine on that cold March day, they, too, will feel panic set in.

I cried harder because I saw clearly what was happening to my life. I would still have my dear mother by my side and my amazing siblings. My husband too was a huge support but none of these people was my father. No one held the place in my heart and in my life that he did. Yes, he was the toughest and hardest to live with, but he was also the one who loved the fiercest, as only a father can. I cried for good reason. As my father left us, my sister sat near him. We took turns in those last hours and she had the privilege of actually seeing him pass on to heaven. And I do mean pass on to heaven. Let me tell you why.

My father had a terribly high fever that caused his body to be almost too hot to touch. He was in a coma of sorts, lying still in his bed. He didn't move, groan, or show any signs of discomfort. But suddenly, he opened his eyes and looked to the ceiling in the corner of his room. He gave a delighted gasp and the nurse sitting near him said, "Wally, what do you see?" My sister ran to his side from the adjacent room. He drew one last big breath and he was gone.

There is no question in my mind that my father saw heaven. Or God or Jesus. It doesn't matter. He saw glory and that gives me hope. I need to know that he is safe and restored, I want to picture him with his sound mind again (he can lose the temper though) and laughing. I need to see him again, to say thank you, dad, just one more time. I need to tell him that, although I'm sure he failed in many ways as a father and a husband, he did more than a good enough job. He worked hard for us, he loved us, and that meant everything.

Fathers need to see themselves the way their children see them. You are, whether you know it or not, the center of their world, the hub of the wheel that is your family, the hero they depend on. If you're not there or not engaged, they suffer.

Missing Heroes

Recently, I heard of a man who had six children by six different women, and he didn't know any of the children. They had become adults and when a friend asked why he never saw them or reached out to them, the man said, "There's nothing that they need from me now." How terribly wrong he was.

Every child needs a father; and that includes grown children. When a father is absent from children's lives, they want to know why. Did he just not care? Or, as they frequently (and wrongly) assume, did they somehow drive him away? The wounds left by an absent father are profound, because dads who go missing are heroes who have gone AWOL.

There are degrees of absence, of course. We have an epidemic, unfortunately, of fatherless homes, of fathers, like that man I mentioned, who don't care about their children. But even more we have an epidemic of homes where dads have been marginalized, either through divorce or even more commonly in households where dad is kept on the periphery. He goes to work, he comes home, and he assumes his children want to spend their time alone or with their mother, so he retreats to his den or man cave and watches TV.

There's a misconception that mothers are the center of a child's world. Mothers are vitally important—I'm the mother of four children myself. But too often we have the idea that fathers are optional, and that often the best thing for them to do is just to stay out of the way. They might be needed as a breadwinner, or to take care of the "honey-do" list, or maybe to discipline the children occasionally, but for the most part many people assume that it is mom who is and should be center stage.

But the fact is that the human family was meant to have mothers and fathers working together, and when they work together, as they were designed to do, their children's lives are enriched emotionally, spiritually, intellectually, and, I can say as a pediatrician, even physically. Children from intact families have a much better chance to be healthy and happy children.

I'll say it again—moms are absolutely necessary, *but so are dads, and to kids it is dads who are the center of the family.* Mom might bend a sympathetic ear or bandage a scraped knee, but dad is the one they want to look up to as the hero who can meet any challenge thrown at the family. And guess what? You dads are wired to handle that pressure, to meet those challenges, to provide for and protect your family.

Let's look at what happens to children when you bear that pressure for the family. Children with stable, involved fathers:

- Have much higher levels of self-control, confidence, and sociability[1]
- Are far less likely to engage in risky behaviors as adolescents[2]

- Are far less likely to have behavioral or psychological problems[3]
- Are far less likely to be delinquent (this is especially true in low-income families)[4]
- Do better on cognitive tests and get better grades[5]
- Are more likely to become young adults with higher levels of economic and educational achievement, career success, occupational competency, and psychological well-being [6]
- Studies suggest that fathers who are involved, nurturing, and playful with their infants have children with higher IQs, as well as better linguistic and cognitive capacities [7]

Clearly, when you as a father engage with your children, teach them, hug them, play with them, and support them, the message they receive is that they matter. When children feel that they matter to their fathers, their world feels safer, more secure; they feel protected. Social science and medical research can give us reams of statistics about how kids prosper in a family with a mother and a father, but I've also seen it, every day, for more than thirty years of working with children and their parents. I have seen thousands of children grow up—some with fathers, some without; and there is an enormous difference.

Daughters who grow up without their fathers are more likely to feel "unsafe" and seek comfort from other, older men, who often use them and then abandon them. Fatherless girls can grow up too fast. They often pursue serial boyfriends, seeking security and affirmation. Instead, they often suffer lasting scars of insecurity, abuse, depression, and disease. As a father, if you care about your daughter, you cannot leave her; you have a necessary role to protect her and show her what a man is supposed to be.

Fatherless sons are more likely to feel anxiety and are at greater risk for depression; if they're the eldest in the family, they will often take on burdens that their father was meant to bear, and it can be too much for them. Giving sons too many burdens too soon, which can happen in fatherless families, means that they are children who miss out on childhood, and the many benefits that come from it. They too need protection; and they also need an ideal of manhood to aspire to. That comes from a hero dad.

A Son, a Tractor, and a Broad Set of Shoulders

When Seth was eleven, his mother began losing her temper with him. He remembers a vivid change in her demeanor. At the time, he thought that he was doing something terrible to provoke his mother's episodes of rage, but he couldn't figure out what. He told me that he would be sitting at the kitchen table doing homework and his mother would walk into the room and start criticizing him for being a bad son. Why? He wasn't sure. She would yell at him for being messy, for being mean to her, or for getting bad grades. None of these accusations made sense to him but they hurt just the same.

Seth lived with his mother and father along with a younger brother on their family farm. His father worked the farm and the days were long—especially during the summer harvest months. When the apples and cherries were peaking, Seth went to the fields and helped his father. He said that he loved being in the fields with his dad running the cherry shaker. He liked being with him even though they spoke little as they worked.

For the first two years of his mother's changed behaviors, Seth said nothing to his father. He knew that his father was stressed because of the farm and work and he didn't want to burden him. Besides he still wasn't sure that his mother's outbursts weren't his fault. She screamed more at him than at his younger brother, so he thought that if he behaved better, she might stop yelling. This never happened.

Then Seth began to pay attention to conversations that his father had with his mother late at night. He heard him trying to reason with his mother. But he couldn't. She yelled at him too and Seth could hear the exasperation in his father's voice. Night after night, month after month, he heard his father trying to calm his mother down but it never seemed to work. At least he knew that his father was aware of the problem.

By the time Seth was thirteen, his mother became violent and began hitting both him and his father. She rarely seemed to be in a good mood but he noticed that she was sleeping more during the day. He was confused and frightened—not just of her but for her as well. What was going to happen to her? What was going to happen to their family? Seth took on much of the household chores like cooking and cleaning and coached his younger brother to do the same. He noticed that his father was spending less time working the farm and more time in the house. This made Seth worry more. How would they make money if his father wasn't working the crops?

Finally, Seth's father sat him and his little brother down one evening for a talk. He said that it was serious. Seth's mother had been diagnosed with a mental illness and was going to be hospitalized for several months. It was going to be expensive. He told his sons that he had tried as hard as he could to help her on his own but he had failed. Seth realized as his father spoke that his father was doing far more to help his mother than he realized. He was trying to protect his sons and in that moment Seth felt grateful for his father.

"We must do something hard, boys," his father said. "We need to sell the farm to pay for the medical care for your mom." Seth's heart sank. He began to cry. Was he crying for his mother or over losing his home? Or was he crying because he felt so badly for his father? Probably all three.

Months went by and the farm was sold. Seth's father bought a very small home on a small plot of land and when his mother had finished her inpatient care, she came home. Life with his mother was better but still not the way it had been when he was young. He missed his old mother. He missed the farm. And he missed working with his father in the orchards. As he grew older, Seth told me that his father had saved their family.

"He is without question, my hero. My father sacrificed everything for our family. The weight of my mom's illness was huge, but he took it. I know that we were hurting financially but my dad refused to let on how bad off we were. And my brother and I were scared. My dad knew it and he did everything he could to keep us calm. There was so much more going on that we never knew about and I guess, looking back, I'm glad he limited what we knew. He protected us. I just hope I can be a man like that one day."

The Difference between Moms and Dads— and Why They're Better Together

In my lectures, I tell parents something that doesn't always sit well. Children respect their mothers, but they see dad as the authority figure—and dads, that's a heavy responsibility. Children will confide in their mothers, but they speak more carefully to their fathers, and the tone is usually more reserved.

There are many reasons for this—and some of them are physical: dad is big and imposing and has a deep voice. But there are deeper reasons too. Many young children see mom as a permanent fixture in their lives. They believe that their mothers *have to* love them and stay with them. That's why many children can be so cruel to their mothers, because they assume mom will never leave; a mother's love is non-negotiable.

But many children don't feel that way about dad; they feel they have to earn their father's love. So they try harder to behave around dad. They don't want to get on his bad side and risk losing him. As a father, you might be totally committed; you might have a cheerful, generous, welcoming personality. But your children will still think they need to earn your respect and love. And that's a good thing, because when children respect their fathers, it makes for a healthier home life. Children tend to behave better when dad's at home—respecting his authority and wanting to keep in his good graces.

Many men feel they have failed as fathers and carry no authority. How could they, they assume, when they drank too much, or couldn't keep a steady job, or were divorced by their wives? In fact, many mothers divorce their flawed husbands because they think they are setting a bad example for the children. But unless those dads have been physically or emotionally abusive, children still want their fathers in their lives—even if their fathers are ne'er do wells. Kids need dads. That's *all* kids, but we know especially that children from low-income families do better—behaviorally, academically, in every way—when dad's around. The key factor is not how much money dad makes, or whether he drinks or has a temper, but how involved he is with his family.

Children and teenagers are fundamentally egocentric. They want the attention of their parents—and they really aren't as concerned about a parent's well-being as most parents believe they are. Kids tend to think of their own happiness, not their parents', and this is normal. And above all, they want the safety of a happy home where mom is there to help and dad is there to protect.

Children don't care if their parents are stuck in an unhappy marriage. They don't think of their parents as husband and wife, but as mom and dad. Mom and dad might be "happier" after a divorce (though that's often not the case) but their children aren't; they usually feel that the bottom has dropped from their worlds. They are confused, angry, and anxious. Many of them grieve as if one of their parents had died. In 99 percent of the cases that I have seen, there is no question that children are happier with two unhappy married parents than they are with a family divided by divorce. Children want to be—and rightfully are—focused on their own happiness, not that of their parents. When they worry about mom and dad, they take on more pressure than they can stand.

A Father Doesn't Have to Be Perfect

Many fathers are intimidated by their responsibilities; they fear, if they have daughters, that they know nothing about how to raise girls; with sons, they might feel handicapped if they themselves didn't have a good father as a role model. Many fathers are perfectionists; they feel that if they're not excellent, they're terrible; and if they think they're terrible, they tend to withdraw from the family.

Fathers have confided in me that when they first held their babies they felt terrified, as well as incapable, inadequate, ill-equipped, and even stupid. Rather than ask for help, they relegate baby care to their wives, because they don't want to risk failing as a father. Don't do this, dads. Here's why.

Most mothers feel the same way. I was in medical school when our first child was born. My pediatrician told me that since I wanted to go into pediatrics, there was nothing he needed to tell me about child care. I almost burst into tears. Becoming a mother is an overwhelming experience, full of emotion and full of fear; and if you feel the heavy weight of responsibility as a dad, so does mom.

What if I couldn't feed my daughter? I had never breastfed before. What if I dropped her, didn't hear her cry at night, forgot about her in the back seat of the car and she suffocated? What if she choked, stopped breathing, or got a high fever? I was almost a physician and I believed deep down that I really didn't have what it took to be a good mom. And my husband didn't feel any better. He was working all the time and worried about not bonding with her.

So if you are afraid and feeling inadequate, welcome to the parents' club. Most of us feel that way—even pediatricians.

The key thing is not to give up or feel like you're not needed. No, you don't have to learn to breastfeed. You might understandably feel that your wife is more adept at changing diapers, and dressing, and bathing, and caring for the baby. Mothers naturally tend to take over—and can be very particular about how things are done, what clothes are put on, and how the car seat is situated. But your wife still needs you, needs your help, even if in the early days you often feel like you're taking orders. Babies need to bond with their fathers as much as with their mothers. Hold your infant as often as you can. And believe me—you, your wife, and your child will be the happier, in the end, the more you are involved.

A Dad and a Mom Moving Forward

When Adam was born, Joseph was overwhelmed. He remembers seeing Adam for the first time and having feelings that felt foreign, powerful, and confusing. He had grown up as an only child with both parents working full time outside the home. He loved his parents but didn't feel close to either of them.

When Adam was born, he was determined to have a very different relationship with his child. No matter what, he said, he wanted a close-knit family—one that enjoyed being together, communicated well, and depended on one another. Mostly, he said, he wanted to be available for his child.

But at that first glance in the delivery room, he felt something inside of him unravel. "I can't possibly be for this child what he needs me to be," he said. I told Joseph that all dads have to learn, but that he had plenty of time, and eventually being a dad would come naturally.

Joseph and Elayne had a good marriage and both wanted to be great parents. When Adam was born, Elayne felt excited and nervous, but much more comfortable in her role as a parent than Joseph did. As the weeks progressed, Joseph noticed that Elayne was withdrawing from him. She would spend more time in bed during the day saying that she was simply exhausted. She would take Adam to their bedroom and the two would stay there for hours. When Joseph tried to relieve her and take the baby away, she became irate.

Elayne suddenly didn't want to see family or friends. She wanted the house quiet and she wanted to be alone. She slept poorly at night, more frequently during the day, and Joseph didn't know what to do. He worked the afternoon shift so he saw what was going on all day until 3 p.m. His wife seemed to be a different person. She became angry and hostile toward him and said that she wanted a divorce. Life felt overwhelming.

Joseph brought Adam in for his two-month well baby check and relayed what was happening at home. Elayne had never acted this way before and he felt desperate for help. I recommended that she see her doctor because I was suspicious that she had post-partum depression. Her doctor confirmed the diagnosis and she got appropriate help. Over the next six months, with help from friends and family, Elayne overcame her depression. Joseph said that those early days as a father, dealing with Elayne's depression, was one of the worst times of his life.

"Not only was I feeling inadequate as a father, I couldn't seem to do anything right for Elayne. No matter what I did, I felt it was wrong. But then I realized that her criticism of me came from her depression, not her real self."

During her depression, Joseph stepped in and took over almost all of the care of Adam. He fed him, bathed him, took him to the store, and got up with him during the night. He got very little sleep during those months between caring for Adam, doing his job, and trying to help Elayne. But things finally did get better.

"In a way," Elayne later told me, "I think that Joe and I were kind of grateful for my depression. Joe and Adam have a bond now that I don't think they would have had if I hadn't gotten sick. Joe calmed Adam during the night, fed him, rocked him to sleep, and he came to see that he really could be a great dad. The two are inseparable now, you know."

Adam was ten years old when Elayne and I had this conversation, and he loved being with his dad. In fact, if something was wrong at school, Adam wanted to talk to his father, not his mother. When he had an afternoon free, he wanted to go hiking or fishing with his father. "Sometimes I find myself getting jealous. I hate to admit this and I'm glad that Joe is so invested in Adam but I often feel excluded. I know they don't mean to, but sometimes Adam and Joe seem to live in their own worlds."

"Are you really *excluded*?" I asked.

"Well, I guess, now that I think about it, no. It's more like I just envy their strong bond; I guess you could say I'm still a little insecure. And, yes, I know I should cherish Adam's strong attachment to his dad. I don't need to compete with it. Our goal is a strong family—and we've got that. We go on family vacations, I go to Adam's hockey games, and I couldn't ask for a better son. Our own relationship is great; it's just that my husband's is greater—and I'm jealous!"

Adam was an emotionally sound and happy little boy who was affectionate with his mother every time I saw them together. I was also glad that Elayne frankly acknowledged both her insecurity and her understanding that she had nothing to be insecure about.

When I told many woman friends that I was writing this book, they told me I was wrong about fathers. They said that men aren't the hub of steel, mothers are. That is inevitably true when fathers walk away; no one can doubt the strength of successful single mothers. But it's not true when fathers are engaged. And if you're reading this book, you almost certainly want to be engaged. How do you do that? All you need to do is to try. This whole book will show you how, but here are a few initial ideas to get you started on being the hero your family needs.

1) *Be tough enough to bear the weight of family burdens.* Many men become frustrated by their wives and children. I get it: you often think you're not needed. But the truth is that you *are* needed. Stay calm and focused and be the man who always steps up for your

family. If your wife asks you to be more helpful at home, be more helpful. If she complains that you aren't doing things right, keep trying, and ask her what she wants. Be tough enough not to react to her criticisms of you and privately, gently ask her to not criticize you for doing your best—especially in front of the kids—just as you promise to refrain from criticizing her when she's trying to do her best. Marriage is a partnership; you need to work together.

2) *Reduce friction.* Where there is discord, you need to bring peace. Men are great problem-solvers; apply your common sense to your family. When children look at their dad as a hero, they're looking for a model of quiet strength, calm confidence, and self-control. When kids and teens have temper tantrums and scream, they are out of control—and they know it, and they know it's a weakness, and they don't want to see the same from you.

3) *Act on your highest beliefs.* The overwhelming majority of fathers I've met want to do the right thing—and in their hearts they know what that is. So I tell them, simply act on it. You have a vision of what a good father looks like. It might be your own dad; or it might be a higher ideal if your dad wasn't present in your own life. Whatever that model is, keep it always in your mind and try to live up to that standard. All of us in the working world know what "professionalism" is; we need to approach our role as parents the same way—acting according to the standards of behavior we expect of ourselves as fathers and mothers, and more than likely that standard—especially for you, dad—is the standard of a hero.

Heroism can mean saving a man in combat or rescuing someone as a firefighter. But there are also less dramatic ways to be a hero, and one way is to be the best dad you can be. Every child wants his dad to be a hero, and every dad has it within him to be a hero to his children.

CHAPTER 2

Who Says
You're Great?

I f I could teach dads one thing, it is this: whether you are a first
time father, a single dad, or a stepfather, being a great dad will
come naturally—if you let it, if you're open to it, if you try, and
if you keep trying when things get hard or after you make a mis-
take.

Too often, fathers assume that they have two left feet when it
comes to being a dad. Our culture has taught them this. For decades—
at least since the 1970s—our popular culture has celebrated women
and moms and told us that dads are clumsy oafs—uptight, largely
unwanted, and mostly unnecessary. Feminists (I confess I was an
ardent one) deserve a big share of the blame for this.

I attended a women's college in the 1970s. We wanted everything we thought men had—more job opportunities, higher salaries,

and even, for some, the "freedom" to be promiscuous. We were determined to beat men at their own game, whatever that game was, and many of us succeeded, or thought we did.

We fought a battle of the sexes without remembering that battles leave casualties—and we certainly did leave casualties. At the time, we weren't thinking of our future spouses, or our sons, or really even our daughters. We weren't thinking of how divorce and promiscuity and endless criticism of men and a denial of their importance in the home would leave a lot of wreckage. After thirty years of working as a pediatrician, I can say without a doubt that the sexual revolution was a disaster for kids—with families far more fractured and fragile than they were before and with kids far more endangered physically, through an epidemic of sexually transmitted diseases, and emotionally, because of a breakdown of the nurturing bonds kids need.

Today, more than 70 percent of African American children live in fatherless homes; so too do about 45 percent of white and Latino children. Those statistics represent a social disaster.

In our culture, dads aren't considered great—in fact, in many cases, they're hardly even around. But that ignores a crucial fact that even these statistics haven't dented: every child believes his father is a great man.

That's what your children want you to be; it's what they expect you to be; and I can tell you as someone who has worked with thousands of fathers, you can be that man.

I know, I know: I've had countless dads tell me that their kids would never call them "great." Kids and teens can be snarky. They can throw tantrums and call you names. But they do that precisely because they need you and love you. And it hurts them when they think you don't care or are not involved in their lives.

Behind closed doors at my office, kids tell me that they cry when dad yells at them, because they desperately want dad to think they're wonderful; they tell me that they think of you, dad, as the strongest, smartest man there is. They think of you as a great man—they think of you as a hero, *their hero*—because you are *their dad*; the one authority figure they want to please more than any other; not their mother, not their coach, not their teacher—*you*.

Daughters have told me in one breath that their fathers drive them crazy and in the next that they feel safer when their fathers are home. Sons have told me that they get terribly nervous when their fathers show up to their baseball or soccer games but if those same fathers don't show up, they feel unloved. These are children (in cognitive terms even eighteen-year-olds are children) and they are confused about many things. But they are not confused about who you are to them.

More than anything else, they want your approval. They're learning from you all the time, from the moment they're born—and for the rest of your life. They want to meet the standard you set for them, because you will always be their dad.

You Are Being Watched

We all know children are mimics. But when it comes to dad, there's more to it than that. They study you every moment you're around, your body language and your tone of voice. They hang on your words. They need to know what *you* think and feel about *them*. Your good moments count—and so do your bad ones. For dads this can be scary. But your influence for good is enormous.

My husband makes regular medical mission trips to South America, and I remember one time when our son—who had never been on a mission trip with him—was debating with his sister about whether he should go. He said he had no interest in medicine, and the trip took up too much time, and it would be hot and uncomfortable. But his sister cut him off. "You need to go because you need to see dad work." Seeing her dad working at a missionary clinic had made a huge impact on her. She saw him stumbling with Spanish (in which she is fluent). She saw him doing his best to help other people. She saw how he dealt with all sorts of circumstances that they would never see at home.

Our son went and had a similar experience (and gained a terrific fund of stories about boat-boarding sloths, giant ants, and snakes falling from trees—experiences that will be with him forever because of his dad). Most of all he saw his father working, striving to help others—he saw his dad as a hero.

As a father, everything you do casts a giant shadow.

It's inevitable. Your son or daughter sees you differently than you do. You think of yourself as a flawed, normal man—or maybe even less than that. But they see you as a hero, a great man whose praise is worth having. They will want to emulate you because they see goodness where you might not. My daughter saw my husband's goodness; she saw how he helped others—and it made a huge impact not just on those he helped, but on her, and then on her brother.

Every day that your children see you, they're shaped by you. And equally important, they're also shaped by your absence when you're not there. So be very careful. You are the giant in their lives. For good or ill, you are not only great, you are larger than life. When children look at their father they want to see the kindest, smartest, strongest, greatest man on earth *who loves them and respects them and is interested in them; that is part of your greatness.*

Now, perhaps you didn't have a great dad at home. Perhaps your parents were divorced and you rarely saw your father. Chances are, you missed him desperately, and you might be bitter that he wasn't there for you and for your mom. So you want to be better than he was and that's not a bad thing. But again, be careful. I've talked to many fathers who have never gotten over the absence of their own father and have taken it out on themselves. When sons don't get to meet the expectations of their fathers—because their fathers weren't there—they can be saddled with a life-long sense of failure, of failing to meet a standard that boys and men expect to be set for them. An absent father can leave a hollow feeling that can never be filled. You cannot change your past, but you can be the best, most engaged dad you can be. Your future belongs to the decisions you make now about the sort of man, the sort of father, you want to be and are going to be.

How Dads Make Time Stand Still

Every minute you spend with your children multiplies in their minds. I remember how one teen told me, "When my dad was around, he and I talked for an hour every night before I went to bed. I miss him so much and I miss those times together."

Another child told me how he and his father had the greatest times going fishing almost every weekend in the summer.

It turned out that these stories weren't quite right. The mother of the teen said, "No, they didn't talk every night. He sat on the edge of her bed every other week or so, when the mood struck him, and they chatted for fifteen or twenty minutes, not an hour."

The father of the boy said he *wished* he could have taken his son fishing every weekend, but it had only been about four times at a local lake. "I'm surprised," the father said. "They were just outings, not even whole days."

I've heard stories like these hundreds if not thousands of times. Do children *lie* about time spent with their father? No. What happens is that when a father spends meaningful time with a child, the experience is magnified. As a father, you have the power to make time stand still. It's the power to make fifteen minutes every other week seem like an hour of every night, or to magically turn four fishing trips into a full summer's worth of fishing.

You alone have this power. I have never heard children talk this way about teachers, or about other people who play important roles in their lives. It's all about dad, because nothing is more important to children than acceptance and affirmation from their father.

Even "Bad" Dads Can Be Great

Even if you've been called a "bad dad," your children will still want your approval. Whatever your circumstances, your role in your children's lives stays the same. Fatherhood, like motherhood, is forever.

Too often I hear divorced parents criticize their former spouses in front of their children. No child should ever hear her mother call her father "worthless" or "stupid." Likewise no father should ever call a child's mother "crazy" or a "slut." Mothers and fathers are icons in children's lives that deserve respect no matter what.

Children want to love their parents. Children expect their mothers to be sources of unconditional sympathy and affection who are always there for them.

With fathers, sons want a role model of what it means to be a man; daughters want their father's affection because it builds their self-esteem.

When divorced parents criticize each other, children often blame themselves for whatever went wrong. On the one hand, they know they need mom and dad. On the other, they know that what mom and dad say is usually right. And when they say bad things about each other, children get caught in the middle.

Unless mom or dad is abusive, every child needs his mother and his father whatever frailties and shortcomings each might have. Volumes of data show how poorly children do when fathers aren't around—and they don't categorize fathers according to personality, job, income, or character. Every child needs her dad even if mom thinks he's a jerk. And every child wants to see his mom even if dad thinks she's crazy. As a dad, you set the example for treating women with respect, just as mom sets the example, or should, for respecting fatherhood.

When Maggie was pregnant with her fourth child, her husband Steve lost his job. He loved being a high school teacher and knew that finding another teaching job in their town would be hard. He became depressed and felt lost. After Maggie had her baby, Steve drank more frequently—sometimes all day.

When Maggie told me about Steve's drinking she broke down sobbing. "I just don't know what to do. I have four small children, no job, and a husband who stays at home all day and drinks. Mostly, I'm worried for the children. It isn't good for them to see their dad drunk. He isn't ever mean, he's just sloppy. They're embarrassed to have friends over. I want to divorce him because I don't want him to be a bad influence on the children."

Maggie was mild-mannered and soft-spoken. She loved being a mother and had sacrificed a lot—including her career as a nurse—to stay at home with the kids. Family was her priority, but now, let down by her husband, she thought divorce was her only answer.

I told her that divorce was no answer at all. "If you get divorced, Steve will have the kids on weekends and you won't be there to help. I know you're angry at him, but the kids don't see a drunk—or not only a drunk—they see their father, and they still want and need his love."

Maggie stayed with Steve, but often felt like a single mother. Steve had periods of sobriety, but always ended up falling off the wagon.

Once the children were in school, she went back to work full-time. The kids progressed and started going to college. When her youngest daughter was a senior in high school, she and Maggie moved out. Maggie had had enough. The marriage was over. Steve drank more heavily after she left.

A few years later, Maggie died of breast cancer. I had the opportunity to speak with her children. Her son said, "My mother was my hero. Through every hardship, she never criticized my father. She knew that we needed and wanted him. I don't think many mothers could have done that. Because she never put him down, we were free to love him. We do love our dad. That's the crazy thing. We love him. I call him periodically to check on him. He's my dad."

Maggie never wavered in her commitment to her children. She swallowed her anger, bitterness, and hurt and left her children a legacy. She taught them how to love people who seem unlovable and to honor their father no matter what.

Steve's story with his children isn't finished. He looks like a bad father and many would dismiss him as a jerk. But his kids don't. They see him through their mother's eyes. And she taught them that however troubled he was, there was good inside of him. They couldn't depend on that goodness but she showed them it was there.

The children don't expect a restored relationship with their father, but they hope for it, because they know the story isn't over yet and miracles do happen; and they're ready for that miracle, because *every* son and daughter with a broken father yearns for a fresh start. And with them, you always start at the top.

Live Like a Hero

When kids enter your life, you don't have to earn their respect. As their dad, you have it. From the moment they set their eyes on you, they admire you and see you as a bastion of strength and authority, and, unless you show them otherwise, of courage and heroism. You might not feel like a hero but my exhortation to you is *live like you are one*. Be the man *they* want you to be; it is, more often than not, the man *you* want to be—and can be.

One of the first qualities your children see in you is that you're tough—strong enough to take on the world on their behalf. Sometimes, especially in the teenage years, that strength will be tested, because they'll want to find out just how tough you are, just how much you care.

Concetta grew up in a home with sixteen kids. Not all sixteen lived under the same roof at the same time, but generally five to ten did. Her parents, Henry and Alicia, took in foster children, and then adopted them. Concetta was adopted when she was five. We talked before she went to college, and by that time she could barely remember her life before adoption. But the few memories she had were terrible.

She did vividly remember moving into her new adoptive home. Though that home would be a godsend to her, she remembered how scared she was when she first arrived.

"I remember when I first came to Henry and Allie's. I was so afraid. Their house was enormous—filled with noises and bedrooms upstairs and down. I had never lived with brothers or sisters. It was overwhelming.

"Mostly, I was afraid of Henry. I wouldn't look at him. I didn't want him to touch me. The idea of him holding my hand or hugging me gave me the creeps." She shook her head in amazement. "Can you imagine? I was honestly afraid of him."

I could easily imagine, because her reaction was that of an abused child, which she had been. I met Concetta when she was six. She was frail, fearful, and shy. She had, in her previous home, been abused by her mother and her mother's boyfriend. As a result, she found it difficult to trust anyone. She rarely made eye contact during those early visits. When I asked her questions, she would nod or shake her head. Occasionally she gave me a blank stare. It was two years before she spoke to me. By the time she was ready for college, she had been completely transformed. She talked easily about everything, especially of the debt she owed her parents, especially her father.

"My dad is one tough man, Dr. Meeker. You know what he put up with—not just me but my brothers and sisters too. It's a miracle that somehow in the last ten years he hasn't had a heart attack with the pressure we put on him."

As a young teen Concetta had angrily expressed the pent up anger she felt against men, herself, and life in general. She chopped her hair off. She pierced body parts. She got a tattoo. When her father discovered her pierced tongue, he was angry—but in a self-disciplined, subdued way—and hurt.

"I'll never forget the look on my dad's face when he saw my tongue bar," she said. "It felt devastating. I was disturbed because he was sadder than he was angry. I knew that I would be in trouble and I'm sure that's half the reason I did it. I wanted to see if he cared. Really. Well, I found out. He didn't yell. He simply took my phone away because he had repeatedly told me that these kinds of piercings were not allowed in our home. They were against family rules.

"He looked right into my eyes that day. He lowered his voice, told me to hand over my phone and his eyes filled with tears. I had really hurt him. It would have been so much easier if he would have yelled at me. But he never yelled at any of us. What was wrong with me, Dr. Meeker? I knew I was hurting him, but I just kept hurting him more. And then I hooked up with that creep. Do you remember?"

I sure did remember.

At fourteen, Concetta found a twenty-year-old man who worked at a local garage. She snuck out at night to meet him. Twice she thought she was pregnant.

One morning she came downstairs to breakfast. Henry saw she had a black eye. "He never yelled at us, but this time he screamed—in shock, I guess, and agony," she told me. "He literally jumped up from the table and pounded his fist on it. I was really scared. I knew that I had pushed him to the brink and he would let me have it. It was finally here—the moment when even my father would show me that he really didn't love me after all. I had screwed up too much for him to love me anymore. I closed my eyes and waited for him to grab me and shake me."

I had heard about the creep, but I had never heard this part of the story. Concetta paused and sobbed.

"Dr. Meeker, you won't believe what happened. He came over to me and gently threw his arms around me. He didn't say a word. He hugged me. Then he hugged me longer. I came up to his chest and I could feel his heart racing. I knew he was going to cry and I didn't want him to. I wanted him to hate me, to grab me, and tell me how horrible I was and drag me out of the room.

"I began crying uncontrollably. The longer he hugged me, the longer I cried. I honestly don't remember how dad and I got to the living room but we did. Maybe he picked me up, I don't know. But we spent hours—honestly, it was half the day—sitting on the couch talking. Mostly it was me. He asked questions and I did the talking and the crying. I don't remember what either of us said but I'll never forget the end of the conversation. My dad took my little hands in his gigantic ones. He looked me straight in the eyes. 'Concetta,' he said. 'You are my precious daughter.' He drew those words out— MY…PRECIOUS…DAUGHTER—just like that. 'You will never again put my daughter in the way of a cruel man. Do you hear me? You are worth far more than a jerk like that.'

"After that day, I felt like a curse was lifted from me. I know this sounds crazy, but that curse was…well…hating men. Hating my past and hating me. Dad taught me to see myself differently. He taught me to see myself as good and to believe that I was good. After that, a light went on in me and my life just turned around. Just kind of simply turned. All because of my dad. Oh I'm going to miss him when I leave for college this fall."

Yes, Concetta, I felt like saying, you are going to miss him. She would carry part of her father with her because he had helped heal her broken little girl heart; he had given her strength. He had been tough enough to face her and to love her when she hated herself and life. He was never cruel and she learned to trust him. By the time she went to college, his strength became hers.

Dads can find daughters a special challenge because they feel they don't understand them. But you don't have to understand your daughter to be a good father to her. You just have to be there for her, to protect her, to guide her, to set rules for her, and to affirm her self-worth by loving her. Henry probably didn't "understand" Concetta; his own life's experiences had been very different from hers; but he was still the greatest father she could have had.

Tough Enough

I have spoken with thousands of fathers who honestly believe that they don't have what it takes to handle a tough teen, a teen like Concetta had been, or worse—but they do, and so do you. It's a cliché, but it's true: men are strong, and you are built to withstand the pressures that get put on you and your family—including the pressure of a rebellious teen. It's one of the reasons that dads get called great, like Henry, when all is said and done.

If you are struggling with a teenage son or daughter right now, let me offer a few words of advice. First, whenever a teenager says "I hate you!" and slams a door in your face, don't take it personally. Teens don't have a lot of self-control, and the person she's really unhappy with is herself. Bad behavior is almost always a reflection of what's going on inside of your teen; it's not about you.

Second, *always* be the grown-up. *You* make the decisions, not him. Have high expectations and make sure he knows what they are. When he yells, show you're in command by speaking softly. That'll impress him far more than yelling back.

Third, sometimes you need to see the little child inside your teen. Dads, because of their natural protective nature, often find this easier with daughters; she's always daddy's little girl. It can be harder to look past a teenage son's six-foot frame and six pack and see the little eight-year-old boy inside. Teenage boys often won't tell you their problems. Instead, they'll hide in their rooms or go out and do dangerous things. But no matter how big he is, or how stubborn and silent he is, or how often he hangs out with his buddies, he wants you to be involved in his life, to show him how to be a man, even to steer him to have the right group of buddies. The fact is, as a teenager, he's lost without you. You might feel inadequate for the challenge; but no son thinks of you that way, and you shouldn't either.

Your Most Important Job Is Your Family

A large part of a man's identity comes from his work. But the most important work, and the most rewarding work, you'll ever have is being a father. A fulfilled life is a life of great relationships, and the greatest relationships are those you'll find with the members of your own family.

As a father, your great talents as a worker are put to their best possible use, because men are, at heart, problem-solvers. Where women are verbal and intuitive and seek insights, men are pragmatic, seek solutions, and take action. A family needs both these skills—mothers who listen and understand, fathers who observe and do. And while fatherhood doesn't come with a paycheck, it comes with emotional and spiritual rewards that surpass any paycheck.

Former NFL wide receiver David Tyree is someone who can testify that family is more important than fame and fortune. David was not only a great football player who made one of the most historic plays in Super Bowl history by catching a pass from Eli Manning on his head, he is a really great dad. Several years ago, he and I were talking about the difference between his life now and when he first started playing for the Giants. In 2003, the New York Giants drafted him. As a professional athlete, his friends and fans assumed he had a great life. He was famous, admired, had a big contract, and was living the dream that millions of young men have, but very, very, very few get to experience. And yet, he wasn't happy.

His life was out of control and he knew it. He drank too much, and in 2004 he was arrested for possession of marijuana. He was putting his health—and his career—at risk.

David landed in jail and experienced an epiphany. While in his jail cell alone for the first time, David told me that he offered an honest prayer to God saying, "Lord, all I know is I need you and if you would allow me to keep my job I would appreciate that too." His aunt soon asked him to go to church with her one Sunday. He went and "By the end of the service," he said, "I was in a pew in the back of the church curled in a ball crying like a child." He said, "The Lord removed my desire for alcohol. And I made the decision to make Jesus my Lord and to pursue a new life."

His girlfriend, pregnant with their second child, gave him an ultimatum expressing she could no longer operate in this unstable relationship. He cut off his other girlfriends and married her in 2004.

They now have seven children, and David is a wonderful dad, deeply involved with guiding his children on the right course, a course he was lucky to find in time, well before he became the Giants' hero of Super Bowl XLII in 2008, when he made one of the greatest catches in NFL history. What is important to know is that a few weeks prior to the Super Bowl, David's mother passed away from a sudden heart attack. He didn't know if he could play in the Super Bowl, he was so stricken with grief. He said that it took every bit of his faith in God to find the resolve to continue on the field. And in the biggest game of his life, he said, "Heaven began to shine over me. I don't even remember grabbing the pass from Eli. The ball just seemed to appear on my head. I just knew I was letting go! People were cheering. Looking back, I am 100 percent certain that the plans and purposes of God were fulfilled in my life on that field." Because of his miraculous catch, the Giants beat the Patriots.

David, as a former football player, obviously is gifted with physical strength, but he also had the moral and spiritual strength to put his life back in order, to put God and family first, and to recognize that money and fame and adulation aren't all that they are cracked up to be. Today, he works with the Giants to assist and equip players with the tools, resources, and information that will promote growth and development on and off the field in their NFL playing experience. The focus is for players to live lives of integrity and to focus on being men of good character, not just football players.

Every man, whether he's a football player or an accountant, needs to tap that inner strength because people are counting on you. In a family, it's the dad who has to have the strength to deal with strong-willed children. Moms, I confess, are more easily manipulated, and difficult children will often take glee in pushing their mothers to get what they want. But strong, pragmatic dads see through this much faster; they recognize challenges to author-ity for what they are—they recognize that strong-willed children are trying to test them, to see what they can get away with; and strong fathers don't let them do it. They don't fail this test of strength. In fact, the wise ones know that if they show quiet strength, they can't possibly lose.

Here is a secret that every parent must know about strong-willed children: they don't want to win. *Really.* They want confirmation of *your* strength, of *your* resolve, of *your* commitment to *them*, because they know that ultimately your rules are all about protecting *them*. They want assurance that you mean it. I'm not saying that these situations don't get messy or that they're not tough, but you don't have to be superman, you just need to be tougher than your stubborn child. Dads are great at that—and if you stand steady, your kids will eventually honor that greatness.

CHAPTER 3

The Leader,
Not the Coach

M any fathers think of themselves as coaches, guiding their sons and daughters to academic and athletic success. Sometimes they go further and volunteer to coach the debate team or the Little League team. And that's great. I'm all in favor of sports (within reason) and bonding with your child that way, but don't fool yourself: a father is not a coach. A father is a leader. And there's a big difference—at least from where I sit. Coaches can teach skills and encourage their execution, but it's a leader who brings vision, which is another way of saying a moral framework for how life is to be lived. That's *your* job—what President George H. W. Bush, who was apparently a pretty good dad, called *the vision thing*.

Moral Leadership

Fathers today have a special challenge, because it's hard to provide moral leadership in a society that has disassembled traditional
moral values, indeed in some cases turned them on their head.

But really moral leadership relies on the same virtue it always
has, and that's moral courage—which means having the intestinal
fortitude to do, say, and believe what you know to be right. That
sense of right and wrong comes from a well-formed conscience—
a conscience that doesn't make up its own rules but that conforms
itself to eternal truth. You might reject that idea of eternal truth,
but it doesn't reject you; you are subject to it all the same. As St.
Paul reminds us, God's law is written on our hearts, and I've seen
it written on the heart of every patient I've ever treated and every
parent I've ever dealt with.

Having a strong moral conscience, a firm idea of what is right
and wrong, is part of being a man, it is part of what defines a hero,
and it is part and parcel of what it takes to be a father who is the
moral leader of his family. It is far less difficult to do that than it
sounds, *because it is naturally part of who you are.* Too often today
we think of morality and right and wrong as indefinable. We think
of leadership as presumption. But that sense of right and wrong
and moral leadership is woven into your DNA and written on your
heart. That's not to say that living a moral life and being a moral
leader isn't hard at times. Of course it is. The very same St. Paul
who said that God's law is written on our hearts also identified
original sin—the fact that even though we want to do good and to
be good, we often do the reverse. The moral life is a battle, but it's
not only a battle *worth* fighting, you *have* to fight it to be the man
you want to be. For your children, it's mostly an unseen battle: they
simply expect you to be a moral leader, and they are right to do so.

Moral courage isn't an option. If you want a close relationship with your children, it's a necessity. Period. Nothing will make or break your relationship with your kids more than this. Stan was a divorced father of three kids: two sons and a daughter. Three years into his marriage, his wife had an affair with a colleague. Stan and his wife went to counseling, but only a few years later she had another affair.

Stan loved his wife very much, but no matter what he did, it was never enough to keep her from having affairs. Finally, she left with her latest boyfriend, divorced Stan, and won dual custody of the children.

As the years passed, Stan felt himself marginalized. His children spent more and more time with their mother. They said their mother needed them and was lonely without them. He didn't force the issue, but he was emotionally crushed.

He lived nearby and was appalled that his ex-wife hooked up with one boyfriend after another, setting a terrible example for the kids.

One day they told him they didn't want to see him anymore. He guessed, correctly, that their mother had poisoned the kids' minds against him. The children were six, eight, and eleven, with the eldest being his daughter. At these ages, children will believe just about anything that a parent tells them, and their mother had taken advantage of that to tell them terrible untrue stories about Stan.

Stan was so heartsick, depressed, and furious at how his wife was separating him from his children that he couldn't sleep, found it hard to concentrate at work, worried constantly, and wrote letters to his children, which he never sent, laying out his side of the story. He didn't send them because he didn't want to do to his wife what she was doing to him. But he wanted to be a bigger part of their lives. He even drove by their home every day, hoping that they would see his car and run to greet him. But they never did.

Instead of venting his emotions publicly, he buttoned them up and tried to *live* in a way that showed that their mother was wrong. He called his children and wrote to them, and was not afraid to tell them that he loved them. On their birthdays, he took them to dinner. Whenever he could, he attended their athletic events and performances at school. He dated but refused to have women stay the night in case his children came over. He never criticized the children's mother. He worked hard at his job and also volunteered for a local charity that helped children in foster care.

Stan lived with moral courage. He kept his feelings about his wife to himself, because he didn't want to complicate his children's already complicated relationship with their mother. He could easily have thrown in the towel, left town, and started a new life. But he didn't, because he didn't want to hurt his kids. For eight years, he lived a life of exemplary self-sacrifice.

During his daughter's first year of college, she asked if he would visit her. "When I arrived at her dorm, I was overcome with emotion," Stan told me. "Elyana was in tears, sobbing. At first I was afraid that something horrible was wrong. Perhaps she was pregnant, or maybe she'd had an abortion. I didn't know because I had been so disconnected from her life.

"When she calmed down, she told me that she had missed me. I wanted to cry but I was afraid to because I didn't want her to focus on me and stop talking. I just let her keep talking. She told me that all those years she often cried herself to sleep worried about me and worried about her mother. She hated her mother's boyfriends. She didn't say anything to her mother about it because her mother seemed so dependent on the children.

"'Dad,' she told me. 'Mom told us horrible things about you—that you didn't love us like she did, that you wouldn't pay for our clothes or school, that you were never good to her. She went on and on about how bad you were. And I just believed her because she's my Mom.'

"But somehow," Stan told me, "my daughter managed finally to get past all that because she missed me and needed me, and saw that I had to be a better person than her mother had said. She needed some help, and thought that I could give it. She looked to me—and it felt great to be back with my daughter."

I'm sure it did. Stan's moral leadership had paid off. It had taken eight years of sacrifice, eight years of moral courage, of setting an example, even from a distance, which eventually brought his children back to him. Kids are drawn to moral courage. We all are. But it's especially magnetic when children see it in the man they want to admire above all others, their father.

A Leader Sacrifices Himself

Stan sacrificed a lot for his children. That comes with being a good parent.

Parents know all about sacrifice—from the pains of pregnancy and childbirth, to sleepless nights, to working hard to support a growing family.

Sometimes the challenges are even greater.

Rick Hoyt was born to his parents Dick and Judy Hoyt in 1962. Rick was diagnosed with cerebral palsy, a condition causing severe muscle spasms, which left him unable to walk or talk. His parents were told to institutionalize him because he was going to be "nothing more than a vegetable." Fortunately, Dick and Judy brought him home and raised him as normally as possible.

When Rick was twelve years old, he was given a device called the Hope Machine that allowed him to communicate with his parents. He told his father that he wanted to participate in a five-mile run in order to raise money to help another teen who had suffered paralysis.

For Rick to "run" the race his father had to run, pushing Rick's wheelchair—and he did. Dick wasn't a runner, but he determined to become one after Rick told him that running the race made him feel like he didn't have a disability.

Dick pushed his 110-pound son in five-mile races, then marathons, and eventually even triathlons that had the pair not just running together, but swimming and biking.

To swim together, Dick strapped his adult son into a raft and roped the raft to his own body. For biking, they had a specially designed bicycle that allowed Rick to sit in front of his father.

Eventually, they competed in more than 950 races, including seventy-two marathons and six Ironman events. Dick said he took on this enormous commitment because he "loved his family" and it made Rick happy.

Dick was not a coach. Sure, he might have given Rick some instruction, inspiration, and direction. But most coaches don't pull a team member through more than two miles of open ocean, peddle a bike 112 miles while bearing a passenger, and then run pushing a wheelchair for more than twenty-six miles. That's not a coach. That's what fathers do for their sons.

Good parents sacrifice their personal time, energy, and comfort for the benefit of their children, expecting nothing in return. In fact, the sacrifice is so natural to them that they hardly know that they're making it. But there's a danger when a parent makes these sacrifices not *for* the child but in order to put the child in their debt.

Mothers might be more prone to this than fathers—I talk to them more often—but it's something to be wary of.

Dick Hoyt represents the first, the good kind of sacrifice. Dick did not run marathons or participate in Ironman competitions because it was his childhood dream. In fact, he told me, many onlookers at races openly criticized him for putting Rick through the stress of racing. What they didn't know was that it was Rick, not Dick, who insisted on competing. He did it, at great sacrifice in time and effort, *for* Rick—purely to make his son happy, not to live vicariously through him, not to control his life, not to seek fame or anything else. He did it *for* his son.

There are, however, parents who sacrifice their time and effort for their children but in ways that are counterproductive. Think of the Little League baseball coach or soccer coach or high school hockey coach who becomes overbearing with his student-athletes and sometimes with others, screaming at them during games, becoming obsessed with winning at all costs (even at a baseball game for six-, seven-, and eight-year-olds). If you were to ask them, they would probably say that they are coaching *for the kids*, but in reality they are doing it *for themselves*. *They* need to feel like winners. *They* need to live vicariously through their children's successes (and are humiliated by their failures). *They* nurture dreams of Bobby or Sally becoming a professional athlete when Bobby and Sally might have no such dreams themselves—or are far too young to think about it and only want to play to have fun, which is what they should be doing. Kids who are coached like this—in over-competitive, over-demanding ways—often end up hating their sport. High school athletes have told me that they feel "used" by coaches and parents who behave like this. And the irony is that the coaches that generate this sort of backlash are often the ones most eager to be seen in the community as someone who "cares" about kids. If they're all about winning, they might say that's because life is all about winning, and kids need to learn that. Actually, life is about a lot more than winning—or at least winning on an athletic field—and most kids know that. It's funny, in a sad way, that parents, of all people, sometimes don't recognize that being a good father, a moral leader, and a godly man, is far more important than being a "winner" in a game, even a big game.

Tangled motives, needy parents, and twisted sacrifices can harm kids—and the kids know it. They feel uncomfortable and they feel uncomfortable because the leadership, the sacrificial leadership, they expect out of you is out of order.

Your kids expect sacrificial leadership out of you, because they think of you as an adult—strong, whole, and complete, intellectually sharp, and emotionally sound—and not growing up and in need of help and guidance like they are. They look to you to have their needs met, not the other way around.

Stephen is one of the most outstanding fathers in my practice. He works as a builder, but he definitely thinks that his most important job is as a dad. Stephen and his wife Alma have a large family, and one of their sons—they had adopted him when he was six—came to the family with serious behavioral problems. Abused and then abandoned by his biological family, Troy refused to let people touch him and could be nasty and violent to his new siblings.

Stephen did what good dads do. He tried to provide Troy with a structured life. He set down the rules of the family. And he tried to hold Troy, and all his children, accountable to them. When Troy became a teenager, his behavior worsened. He flunked out of school. But Stephen and Alma insisted he get a job; and if Troy misbehaved at home, his father didn't yell at him, but instead gave him a list of physically demanding chores to do—from chopping wood to shoveling dirt.

At age eighteen, Troy left home. When he returned, it was under cover of night, while his parents and siblings were on vacation. He broke into the house and stole money and valuables. When Stephen caught up with Troy, and Troy confessed to the crime, Stephen offered him a deal. Troy could either join the military, or his dad would report him to the police.

Troy enlisted in the army, and as his father hoped he would, Troy found the structure and discipline he needed in his life, as well as a sense of direction and some job skills. He also got married (to someone Stephen and Alma like very much) and had a child. Stephen and Alma even invited Troy's wife and baby to come live with them while Troy was deployed overseas in order to ease some of the financial burdens on the young family.

Several years later, I had the opportunity to speak with one of Stephen's daughters, Cecily, who was living in the house at the time. She clearly adored her dad—and even loved the fact that he was strict. It wasn't just Troy who had been disciplined with manual labor like chopping wood. Any boy in the family who stepped out of line got similar treatment. If the girls misbehaved they had to run laps around the house. She said that at times, it was actually fun. But she would never tell her father that.

On the other hand, Cecily said, her father always told them how much he loved them, and he was a kind and generous man. She saw, when Troy's wife and child were living with them, just how much he was willing to sacrifice his own comfort for his children and grandchildren.

Stephen rarely went hunting, fishing, or golfing with friends. He was too busy with his kids. When he did go on vacation, he packed up the whole family. He never took a break from being a dad, or being a granddad. He was totally committed to his family.

And it has paid off for the children, including Troy, who matured in the army, has a solid marriage, now has a good civilian job, and, I am happy to say, finally recognizes what a blessing it was to have parents like Stephen and Alma.

A Leader Doesn't Follow the Crowd

All of us want our children to do well, to have friends, to be liked by their peers. But sometimes we put too much focus on the wrong things. It's great to have a son who is a starter on the baseball team or who excels in chemistry, or a daughter who gets straight A's or who has a wicked spike in volleyball. But it's also not a bad thing if your son sits on the bench but still loves the game or your daughter gets straight B's if that's the best she can do.

What really matters is not these accomplishments, but building character in our kids, because character is about who they really are—not just as baseball players or as students, but as people. Growing in character is something dads help kids do, and your leadership is essential when it comes to helping kids avoid bad peer pressure.

You need to lay down the rules—and to do what you know to be right (because you probably are), no matter what other kids are doing and what other parents allow.

Take cell phone use for instance. Fathers know that too much screen time is bad for their sons and daughters; it can turn their sons into zombie-like video-game addicts or open their daughters to bullying on social media. Without proper guidance, screen time can cause a lot of serious harm to kids; believe me, I've seen it. Dad, you need to be the one to step in, establish the ground rules, and enforce them. And it won't be easy—not when all of Susie's friends want her engaged on social media all the time and not when your formerly trim, tanned athletic son has become a grouchy, pale-faced, droopy-eyed, baggy pants bore whose closest friends are fellow gamers who chat with him over headphones connected to the Internet. Setting electronic limits might hurt their feelings in the short run, but it's better than letting them hurt their lives or stunt their aspirations and potential. As writer Jim Geraghty points out in his rollicking guide to fatherhood, *Heavy Lifting*, co-authored with radio host Cam Edwards: the point is that video games, fun as they are, are simulations of actual experiences. And you shouldn't settle for just a fun, active, virtual life. You're capable of more. To quote every wise mentor character in every adventure movie ever, *you're destined for so much more*. And whatever you're destined for, it's not going to happen with you sitting on the couch, leaning left and right with the console in your hands.

Most fathers, in my experience, readily understand the dangers kids face from electronics and are willing to enforce simple rules regardless of what others might think. Moms have a harder time because they do care what other kids and their parents are doing; they tend to be more socially minded and more connected to their children's friends and parents; and they don't like hurting people's feelings and saying no whenever everyone else is saying yes. Dads, on the other hand, don't mind being the leaders and laying down the law. And that's what you should do. Your family, consciously or not, depends on you for that very skill and virtue.

Dad is the one who can ground his teenage son and not worry about the backlash from the boy's friends. Dad's the one who can tell his wife "My daughter's not wearing that," when mom and teenage daughter know that's the style that other girls are wearing.

The trick, dad, is to stand firm when your wife, your daughter, and your son tell you that you're out of touch, that you need to bend the rules a little, that they'll be unpopular if they can't go out or can't wear that mini-skirt. You're strong enough to say no—and wise enough to understand that no is the right answer. Good leaders do the right thing regardless of what others think.

Joel Jensen coached his son's Little League team all the way to the consolation round of the Little League World Series. Jensen's team from Bend, Oregon, was leading Italy 6 to 0 and Jensen's son Isaiah was pitching. He was clearly wearing out and his pitches had become inconsistent. After Isaiah walked a player, his father ran out to the mound. Jensen didn't know that a TV microphone would pick up his conversation with his son.

He said, "I just came out to say that I love you as a dad and a player. You're doing awesome out here, okay?" Then he said, "Cheer up, have some fun."

Jensen was his son's coach, but in that conversation his more important role was as a father and a leader who confirmed for his son that he loved him—whether he struck out every hitter or walked every man—that he was proud of him, and that this great moment, a Little League World Series game, should be fun. That's a conversation that will live in his son's life forever.

If coach Jensen had reprimanded Isaiah, telling him to "Push harder, concentrate more, don't let your team down," he would have taught a young boy that what really matters is not himself, but what he can do with a baseball. That's the wrong lesson. Joel Jensen taught the right lesson, because he knew that ultimately the game was not about him—not about his team winning or about his being the victorious coach—but about the kids, including his son. For them, sure, it would be great to win. Greater than that is to enjoy the game for the great experience that it is. I know at least one man whose proudest moment as a high school wrestler came not from the few easy victories he notched up, but from a tough, competitive match that he ended up losing.

Sports can indeed teach character. But when they do it is because they actually live up to the old adage of "It's not whether you win or lose; it's how you play the game." Coaches have to coach to win, sure, and to improve their players' skills and sense of strategy. But leader dads have to go beyond that, and teach their sons that character is what matters—the discipline, the dedication, the effort, the commitment, and yes the sense of fair play—all those qualities that can be nurtured in sports and turned to greater ends. And greater than winning—or losing in the great match where you gave it your all and lost—is to know that your dad loves you regardless.

There are many ways that you can sharpen your skills as a leader for your family. Here are a few.

1) *Be bold enough to teach your children right from wrong.* Keep it simple at first, but draw clear lines for your children, such as:

a. It is wrong to hit or harm another person.
b. It is wrong to lie or steal.
c. It is wrong to be disrespectful to older people (and yes, that includes you!).
d. It is wrong to be lazy.
e. It is wrong to do harm to, or to be disrespectful of, your own body—no tattoos, piercings, gorging on food (or the reverse, trying to make yourself impossibly skinny), or taking drugs or smoking or drinking alcohol.
f. It is wrong to neglect your responsibilities like school work and household chores.

Then, be sure to tell them what is right to do:

a. It is right and honorable to tell the truth.
b. It is right to help another person who needs help.
c. It is right to return lost articles to the rightful owner.
d. It is right to treat others as you would like to be treated yourself.
e. It is right to speak respectfully to teachers and other adults (even if you feel they don't deserve it).
f. It is right and honorable to work hard and show pride in your work.
g. It is right to protect your body by exercising and eating healthy food, and (when they're older) to be chaste as a matter of self-respect.

These rules will make your children feel more secure—and even prouder of being your son or daughter.

2) *Act sacrificially.* Leaders always put the welfare of others first—in your case, dad, that means your wife and children. It is crucial to remember that your wife is as equally deserving of your sacrifice as your children. Nothing is more important to give yourself a strong, happy marriage, and to give your children the right sense of perspective, than to treat your wife with deference, respect, and old-fashioned courtesy and chivalry. There is absolutely nothing wrong with being her knight in shining armor, because surely that's the sort of husband you want your daughter to have and the sort of man you want your son to be. The world would be a whole lot better off if parents raised their children this way; if they led sacrificially (and happily) for each other and for the family.

Here are some ways to lead sacrificially:

a. Instead of taking that weekend fishing trip with your buddies, take the *family* on a weekend fishing trip.

b. Ask your wife how you can help with the household chores. (I guarantee your kids will be watching—especially if you make them part of the deal: "What chores can *we* do for *you*?")

c. Take money that you've set aside for a new set of golf clubs—or something similar—and put it into a college savings account for your children.

d. Instead of plopping down on the sofa when you come home from work, take your wife and children to a baseball game or out to dinner, even though you're tired and just want to rest.

e. Instead of coming home and cracking open a beer, come home and open the box of a board game for a family game night. Let your children see you put money in the poor box at church—and encourage them to do the same.

f. Volunteer to do charity work—like serving in a soup kitchen—and bring your children with you.

One of the great benefits of sacrificial leadership is not just doing the right thing, but watching what extraordinary men and women your children grow up to be when they follow your example.

CHAPTER 4

You Aren't Your Dad

If your father was a great guy, like mine was, you have my permission to skip this chapter. You were given a great role model, and that is a wonderful gift to have.

But if you had a tough relationship with your father, I have good news for you: you can still have a happy family life and a great relationship with your children. Many of the football players I work with came from fatherless homes, but they have committed themselves to being the great dads they wanted in their own lives—and they're succeeding.

You can't rewrite your childhood, but you can take charge of your future. And your kids can help, because *they* want a great relationship with *you*. Dads are meant to be heroes to their children—and you start off with that status from day one. So, as they say in football, you have the lead, the game is now yours to lose or to win.

Building a Better Legacy

The challenge is to learn from your bad experiences and not repeat them, or variations of them, in your own family. Sure, we all inherit behaviors from our parents. If your father was a yeller, chances are that under stress you might be too—even if you vowed never to do that. Breaking the pattern of ingrained behaviors can be hard, but it also can be done. Like most things, it takes work; and like most things you have to work at, it's worth it. The first step to becoming a better dad than your own father is to recognize his mistakes and, most importantly, *recognize how they affected you as a boy.* Put yourself back in your little boy shoes and remember how you felt when your dad yelled, or didn't attend your ballgames, or seemed too busy to take any interest in you, or wasn't there when you needed him; or wasn't there at all because he abandoned your family.

I won't presume to guess how you feel about any of those experiences, but I can tell you that whatever you feel is important because it will have shaped the sort of man you are today, and set challenges you might need to overcome.

Boys and Their Missing Dads

In my practice as a pediatrician, boys have told me a lot about their absent or disengaged fathers. Often what they tell me comes in floods of tears. Many, when they're young, construct fantasy fathers to make up for the father they've never seen or rarely see. When they're older, they feel the void in a different way.

Frequently they blame themselves, thinking they must have driven their father away or caused him not to care. Kids care—*a lot*—about their dad, and if your father abandoned you it likely left you with a lasting sense of insecurity and anxiety. Boys—and grown men—want to know whether they're meeting their father's standards.

Boys who have been abandoned by their fathers have a much harder time trusting other people. They have a very hard time with intimacy, because they don't want to risk their feelings again. They can even have problems figuring out how to be a man, because a crucial role of a father is to affirm his son's masculinity in a constructive way.

If any of this describes you—again, there is nothing to be afraid of. If you meet your past head on, you can conquer it in your current life.

One of my challenges to dads is to put their love on the line: prove it. Perhaps your father never hugged you and told you he loved you. Maybe you are scared to death to do that with your own son. DON'T BE. Hug him. Tell him that you love him. It might feel awkward at first; it will be tremendously rewarding later. It will deepen and strengthen—or even restore—the love of your family. Expressing love yourself is one great way to overcome the lack of love you received when you were young. It is one way to prove to yourself that not only are you *not* your dad, but that you can do *better* than your dad.

And maybe, in a different way, you've had that challenge before. If you grew up without a father, chances are you had to grow up quickly. Especially if you were the eldest, you probably had to be the "man of the house." Having a little responsibility can be a good thing, but it has to be age-appropriate. You might have found it overwhelming. Many boys from fatherless homes feel like failures, because they could not do everything they were asked to do.

If you have those feelings, put them aside. If, as a boy, you shouldered a man's work, you should be proud for doing the best you could. As a father yourself, you can make sure that you—not your daughters, not your sons—carry the load that a dad is meant to carry.

Being Man of the House

When Roland's mother was seventeen, she became pregnant with his older brother. She and his father married and about two years later they had Roland. Several years later, they gave Roland another brother and a sister. Roland's childhood was difficult at times. With very little money, his mother moved the kids nearly every year from house to house while his father frequently disappeared—often for weeks at a time. "My father was a really nice guy," Roland told me. "I don't really know what he did or where he went, he was just simply never around. He came around for our birthdays and Christmas but other than that, especially when I was very young, we rarely saw him."

When Roland was seven years old, his mother finally decided that she was tired of trying to explain to her kids why their father was never home so she left him. She went to work outside the home to make ends meet for the family. Roland told me that during his early years, with his father absent, he and his brother became best friends and rascals. They would go to school to get breakfast and then leave school and wander around. When it was time for school to be out, they would find their way home so their mother wouldn't know they skipped school.

"As odd as it sounds," Roland said, "My ten-year-old brother Ronnie was like a father to me. My mother often left him in charge when she was gone." Then one summer, Roland's mother took the four siblings on vacation to Las Vegas to visit family. It would prove to be the worst trip of his life. Shortly after they arrived, his mother and aunt dropped Roland and his siblings along with their cousins at a local pool. Roland remembers his brother acting up and being told by the lifeguard to sit on the edge of the pool. Before he knew it, no one could find his older brother so he and the cousins scoured the park.

Until someone pointed out to the lifeguard that a child was lying on the bottom of the pool. "I remember looking at my brother stretched out on the cement by the pool and people trying to revive him. I had no idea that he was dead. My uncle, a fireman who responded to the emergency call, took us home. I don't remember the ride home. But I do know this: when my brother died, part of me died too. In many ways, it was the death of my boyhood.

"I remember seeing my mother sitting on the side of my aunt's bed sobbing. She looked at me and asked how this happened. I was eight and didn't know what to say. Somehow, I felt that it was my fault. After my brother's funeral, we really didn't speak about him. I guess everyone just stuffed the pain of the experience away." As Roland recounted his story, I wanted to reach out and hug his eight-year-old self.

His mother took them back to Ohio and life went on except this time, something was very different. Not only was his brother-best-friend-father-figure missing, now he had to step into his brother's role. I asked Roland a question that had burned inside me since I began witnessing the phenomenon of boys becoming the "father" in the home after their father leaves. "Did you automatically become the father of the house or did your mother begin treating you as the dad? Which came first—her expectations of you being the father or your expectations of yourself to be him?"

"Both happened but first my mother began putting me in charge in her absence, sort of like a surrogate father of the home. And I accepted it. From the time my older brother died, I was put in charge of my brother and sister. That's just the way life was," he said. "Many times boys in this situation rebel in their teen years because they are tired of living a life that shouldn't be theirs. But I didn't. My mother taught us to work hard and that's what I did. I dealt with my pain and rejection by working."

And work hard, Roland did. He went on to Princeton University and then Wharton Business School. He married his current wife and started a family. His wasn't the only life to take a dramatic turn—so too, did his father's. "My father became a passionate Christian later on. He married another woman and had two more children. He served in the church and became a pillar of the community." But he never reconciled the pain he caused Roland or his siblings.

During his adult years, Roland enjoyed a cordial relationship with his father. Whenever they found themselves in the same town, they met for a meal. His father was never cruel, rude, or demeaning. He was kind to Roland. He told his son that he had become a new man and that he felt that he had started his life over again.

When Roland was in his late thirties, his father died. He would discover that his father's funeral, like his brother's death, would become another turning point for him. "When I went to the funeral, my wife, my sons and I sat in the second or third row behind my father's current wife and kids. People spoke at the funeral and one after another spoke accolades about my father. At one point I saw my step-brother throw himself on my father's casket and sob. But I didn't shed a tear. The church was packed with well wishers and folks who said that my father had changed their lives. One man spoke from the pulpit to say while he was in prison, my father came to him and helped him turn his life around. I began burning inside," Roland said. "I wanted to hit someone. From grade school through college, I had excelled in academics and sports. And, as I heard this man speak, I wondered if I needed to go to prison in order to get my father's full love and attention. I was crushed. The experience was surreal. We—my brother, sister, and mother, were his first life. We should matter. But at his funeral, there was no special mention or even acknowledgment that we ever existed."

Roland put the funeral behind him and worked harder. In fact, he had recently joined the prestigious investment bank Goldman Sachs. One day, a friend asked him to be COO of the National Fatherhood Initiative. He agreed and before he knew it, he was president. As he was preparing to take the stage and give a speech for a community fatherhood program as the new president, the organization showed a film. A graduate student was interviewing children, asking them what it was like growing up without a father. Roland sat in the front row watching when a lovely girl named Joanna answered the interviewer's question. As she spoke, her face changed. She began to lose her composure. Then the interviewer asked her, "If there was just one thing you wanted fathers to know and remember, what would it be?" Her answer became cemented in Roland's mind.

"I would tell fathers," she began, "*you need to love your children.*" And then a single tear rolled down her cheek.

"Suddenly," Roland said, "when I heard her say that, I became unglued. Here I was getting ready to address people on the importance of fathers and all of my own pain that I had hidden for decades welled within me and took over. I was in tears and could barely speak."

Roland has spoken to thousands of men during his career as president of the National Fatherhood Initiative and he has learned a lot about men who grow up without dads. "What people don't realize" he said, "is that rejection from a father is entirely different from rejection by a mother. When a father rejects his son, he lives with a hole in his soul in the shape of his dad. I believe that God whispers to children in the wombs of their mothers that there is a father waiting for them that will love them like no other. And, if this father cannot and will not fill this hole, it can leave a wound that is not easily filled. And, alas, I, like too many others, am a wounded soul."

So, Roland teaches men that if they have experienced father-lessness or father rejection, they will have this hole in their souls. Many men, like him, choose to shove the pain deep inside and cover it with hard work, rebellion, drugs, alcohol, and many other things. He had. "But men have a decision to make" he told me, "that if they want to stop the pain and not dump it onto their kids, they need to face it. Then, they must be willing to break the cycle and they really can." That's what the work of the National Fatherhood Initiative is about—helping wounded fathers under-stand their value in their children's lives and be the best fathers they can be no matter what their relationship was like with their own fathers.

Lack of a Role Model

A friend of mine who plays in the NFL told me a beautiful, but very sad, story about growing up without a father. He loved his mother and knew how hard she worked to take care of him and his five siblings. Every Christmas he wanted to give her the biggest present he could find. It didn't have to be expensive but it needed a large box, something to impress. One year that huge box was a plastic punch bowl set. The next year, because he couldn't find her anything bigger, he gave her another punch bowl set; and the following Christmas, she got another. They didn't do much entertaining, but if they ever did, they were set with punch bowls!

Like my friend who had no idea how to show his mother he loved her besides giving her punch bowls on Christmas, men who grew up without a father often say that they have no idea how to be a good dad—or for that matter a good husband. They never had family dinners, or heard their mother and father talk as a loving couple, or as kind, understanding parents. No father read them bedtime stories or talked to their teachers. They have no role model for how to be a father.

I have enormous respect for my many friends who grew up without fathers but who are determined themselves to be great dads. One great example is Rob Davis, who played professional football for eleven seasons with the Green Bay Packers. Rob and his five siblings were raised by a single mom in a poor neighborhood in Washington, D.C. Growing up in his neighborhood was hard, and "At some point," Rob told me, "I knew that I either would end up in jail or with the NFL. I was clear in my mind which way I wanted to go." Rob went undrafted, but went on to have a very successful career as a long snapper.

When I asked Rob how he learned to become a good father, his answer was simple. It was the example he saw at a friend's home when he was growing up.

"I will never forget sitting at my friend's kitchen table eating dinner with his mother and his father. They were all together and I knew that one day, I wanted that. I wanted to be sitting at a table with my wife and my kids. We would be there, together." That example set the course of Rob Davis's life.

If you didn't have a father yourself—and didn't have the example of another great dad—don't worry. It's easier than you think. If you had bad examples when you were a kid, you know what to avoid. If you had good examples, you know what to emulate. In every case, there is a great father within you, because men are meant by God (I believe) and by nature, for the raising and caring of the next generation, to be good fathers.

Breaking Bad Dad Habits

For most dads the two most common pitfalls to avoid are anger and alcohol. Many men who grew up with bad dads cite their own fathers' lack of self-control, especially when it came to controlling their emotions and controlling their drinking. Let's take each of these in turn.

The Mean Father

Many boys grow up with fathers who, for one reason or another, have terrible tempers. Some men rage at their families and this is terrifying for kids. If you had a father who raged, you know what I mean. When the yelling started, you might have run to hide in your room or a closet—or, if you were older, you might have confronted him, challenging him to stop, and borne the misery of facing him.

A Torn Masculinity

Men who live with a mean or out of control father have a very difficult time. Not only do they feel afraid, demeaned (if the father berates them), and insecure about what will happen next, but they also have difficulty with their masculinity. Boys feel that as a young "man" their job is to protect others in the family who are being hurt. If their father is abusive toward their mother, they hate seeing what is happening to their mother and they want to intervene. But intervening means hurting your father and this puts you in a horrible dilemma. What child, what man, wants to harm his father? He is torn between protecting his mother and siblings (if he doesn't he feels weak and cowardly) or confronting and possibly harming his father (whom he wants to love and admire).

If you had a father who was mean to you, I am so terribly sorry. You didn't deserve it. No child deserves to be screamed at, frightened by the very person who is supposed to protect him. You know that harsh words from a father—words like "idiot" or "worthless" or "stupid"—can cut a child to the quick.

But perhaps you also know, from that experience, the importance of watching your language. You know that everything you say as a father matters, that it is magnified tenfold in the ears of your children. You know that your children deserve respect and understanding as much as you do. You understand that in a child's mind, a father is the wisest man they know. If a father tells a son that he will never make it in life, sports, academics, relationships, or whatever, he'll likely fear his father is correct.

Many men actually choose career paths that will "show their father" they are successful, even if the father isn't paying any attention, even if he's dead. I have watched grown men continue to risk their health, money, and families in order to finally settle a score with their dad.

Good men, you need to remember that you—and your wife and children—are inherently and enormously valuable because you are made in the image of God. You do not need to prove anything to your own dad if he spoke about you in anger or ignorance or in any other unjust, negative way. The Lord's Prayer has it right when we pray that God might "forgive us our trespasses *as we forgive those who trespass against us.*" There is tremendous wisdom in that.

As a family, you should cherish each other, support each other, and respect each other. We should also forgive each other for our failings and missteps, especially when our intentions were well meant. And as a father, as the moral leader of your family, you should use the experience you had in your own family growing up, whether it was good or bad, and apply what you learned from that experience to be a better dad.

Yes, maybe you lacked a role model for expressing respectful disagreement with a wife or disappointment in a child. But maybe you *did* have a role model for what *not* to do—and understanding that can be half the battle.

Just take a step back. Think how, as a boy, you would have wanted your father to address you—and correct you when you had done wrong. Think of how you would have liked your father to address your mother. Hold those mental images and work to be that man. "Kinder and gentler" isn't that hard, if you're committed to it.

As hokey as it sounds, a useful exercise, and actually an enjoyable one for the entire family, is to sit down and watch those old family sitcoms of the 1950s and early 1960s like *Leave It to Beaver.* You want a simple role model for a respectful father and husband? It's a simple YouTube or Netflix click away to Ward Cleaver, the wise, strong, and kindly father in *Leave It to Beaver*. When Jim Geraghty and Cam Edwards were looking for the gold standard of fatherhood in their book *Heavy Lifting: Grow Up, Get a Job, Start a Family, and Other Manly Advice*, that's exactly where they turned—to Ward Cleaver, asking at the end of every chapter: "What Would Ward Cleaver Do?" Good question—and good advice, especially in the art of self-control.

The Alcoholic Father

Mean fathers are often alcoholic fathers, but with additional problems for their children.

Father A and Father B

Children living with alcoholic fathers experience two dads. There is the sober dad and the drunk dad. If a child is "lucky," then his drunk dad is kinder when drunk; but for many boys, their fathers are meaner and more aggressive when drunk.

But more than that, drunks are unpredictable and untrustworthy, which can be frightening for children.

When a father is drunk, you can't depend on him to pick you up after school. You have to make excuses for him. He might embarrass you. You can never relax around him and you don't want to provoke him. You become guarded and wary.

This is hard on boys and it can leave them with a lot of pent-up anger that in turn can lead to depression and a feeling that life is nothing but misery—either you walk and talk warily or you're verbally abused. Like many bad experiences, surviving this experience—if that's what you endured—can be, with the right understanding, a powerful incentive to do better.

You don't want your children to see you that way. You don't want to *be* that way or to burden your children with those sad memories. So don't. Don't seek refuge in a bottle. Don't take out your frustrations on your wife or your kids (or your dog for that matter).

You're a man—so man up. You are a good man who wants to be a good dad. You are strong enough to face any challenge that life throws at you. You're made that way. That's what your children expect, that's what your wife expects, and that's what you should expect of yourself. So be confident, be strong, be the man you want to be. If that means locking up the liquor cabinet, do it. That's a small price to pay for reclaiming your life and saving your family.

How You Can Be a Better Father than Your Dad Was

Even if you grew up with a mean, absent, alcoholic, or disengaged father, you can still be a great dad. Here are a few ideas on how to start.

Figure out what kind of a father you want to be and work toward it. Create a mental picture of your model father. He would probably be home in the evenings to talk with his kids at dinner. He would help them with their homework. He would be patient and show interest in how his kids' days went.

So there you go. That's where you start. Do your best to show up in the evenings and whenever you can during the day. Be home on weekends. Rather than go to the bar to grab a drink with your buddies after work, go straight home. Talk to your kids and ask how their days were. Do they need to go somewhere or do they need help with their homework? Sit down and help. Even if you don't understand a subject like Calculus, listen to their struggles with it. The point is: show up for them the way you wish someone would have shown up for you.

Don't let your past harm your present. It is one thing to *learn* from the bad experiences you might have had as a boy; it is quite another to hold your own children responsible for them—though fathers sometimes do this. A dad will sometimes get angry with, or feel hostility toward, his own sons and daughters because he thinks they're ungrateful for having all the advantages he didn't have.

Obviously your children are not responsible for your past, but it's easy to fall into this trap. The best way to avoid it is to recognize that it *is* a trap, a natural subconscious reaction that you need to guard against. If you find yourself feeling angry or agitated with your kids, ask yourself why? Is it really because of something they have done? Is your anger proportionate to the offense that they have committed? And try this trick as a way to moderate your response: pretend that your child is the neighbor's kid; that takes the emotion out of it and can help you formulate a cooler, more rational, and better reaction.

Remember that you are your own man. There will be times when you find yourself behaving just like your father did. This isn't your fault. It's just life. So realize that it will happen and do your best to change course, if you're following a bad example; and don't be afraid to follow the familiar, familial course if it's a good one.

Trust your instincts. God gave you everything you need to be a great dad. Within you are the strength, patience, and love of a father. So trust your instincts, and do what your gut tells you is the right thing to do, because it usually is.

Play a lot with your kids. Sometimes the best way that men can be better fathers is to give themselves a break and play with their kids. Studies routinely show that kids develop better physically, mentally, and emotionally, and feel more secure when their fathers play with them. Being a father can be—*it should be*—fun for you and your kids. So get out there and play with them. All kids—babies, toddlers, middle schoolers, and even teens—love to play with their fathers. And dads—you'll be happy to learn—are usually better at playing than moms are (unless it's a board game). If you have a daughter, take her to the park, to go swimming or rollerblading, to the zoo, to the movies, or out to dinner. You don't have to spend a lot of money. You can play in the backyard or take a scooter out on your sidewalk. You can shoot hoops with your son or play catch, or run around in the basement, or teach him a new hobby, like making model airplanes. He'll feel like a million bucks because you chose to play with him. If you have a few hours, go for a bike ride, to the park, hiking. Just about anything that gets you out of doors and away from electronic screens is a good thing. One of the many problems with computer or video games, which dads sometimes revert to, is that it pits you against your children; and instead of playing, observing each other, you're side by side, staring at a screen.

The only other warning you need is to make sure your play time is just that, *play time*, and that it doesn't involve serious competition. If you are a competitive person, beware of any sport where the competitive streak in you will come out, because serious competition can destroy the fun, especially for your daughter.

Most fathers forget to play with their kids because they think they "need to get things done," whether it's work around the house, or in the yard, or balancing the bank statements, or keeping up with emails from the office (even on nights and weekends). Don't do this. Nothing is as urgent as or more important than spending time with your family. As physicians, my husband and I have plenty of "urgent" things to do. But guess what, most of them really aren't. For true emergencies, there are emergency rooms. Even for a doctor, most things can wait for normal office hours. So stop. Give yourself a breather—and play. You won't regret it.

Choose happiness. Growing up with a mean father, or without a father, can leave scars. But scars can heal. And much of the stress that fathers put on themselves—because they feel unprepared to be good fathers—is completely unnecessary. Whatever happened to you in the past, when you were growing up, is done. Yes, it has some lasting effects, but as Jesus said, let the dead bury the dead; leave the deadweight of your past behind you. An unhappy past does not preordain an unhappy future. You can still, by dint of your own commitment, have a fresh start at happiness and a great relationship with your kids and spouse. I know this because I've seen it many, many times. The men who do this best are the men who consciously choose happiness for themselves, for their wives, and for their kids. That means ridding your mind of negative thinking. It means living for others. It means doing what is good, right, and noble. It means embracing the idea that fatherhood is not just a responsibility; it is an adventure—and fun—and what you were made for. So make the most of it!

CHAPTER 5

Three Questions Your Child Needs You to Answer

I sat across from Lori sipping thick black coffee.

"Dr. Meeker, sometimes I think back to those days and feel so badly for my dad. I mean, what I put him and my mom through was tough and I feel so guilty."

I thought to myself, "You have no idea, sister," but simply nodded and smiled. Lori was twenty-six now and recalling her life at fifteen. In many ways, I couldn't believe that she and that nasty fifteen-year-old I remembered was the same person.

"Do you think I should talk to my dad about those days? I mean, I think I owe him an apology or something." She blew into the whipped cream and cinnamon that topped her coffee. She looked calm and self-aware in a way that she had never been in her teens. The truth was, she would never fully understand what she put her father through, which was a ton. Even if she became a mother herself she would never fully understand what her father endured, because dads experience things differently than moms do. Mothers bear the brunt of some of their children's ills; fathers bear others, and their suffering can sometimes be much more hidden, much more interior.

"Yes, I think it would be a very good idea if you talked to your father. I think that forgiveness is an enormous part of healing and I know that your dad would love you to ask forgiveness for your part in the troubles."

She looked a bit startled.

"Forgiveness? I was kind of thinking about just letting him know that he did a great job and that I didn't mean to put him through so much. But asking for forgiveness, I don't know about that. I mean, he was wrong too. That's kind of heavier than I wanted to get."

"So tell me what you'd say," I prodded.

For the next forty-five minutes Lori retold a story I knew well. I didn't mind hearing it again because this time she spoke as an adult with a keener awareness of herself and her behaviors.

"Remember when I was fourteen, and I started at the new high school? I was overwhelmed. I felt like a geek—tall, skinny, ugly, and alone. I didn't want anyone to see me. I wasn't one of the smart kids or the jocks. I was just a kid who had no clue about anything. Who does at that age, really?

"Most of my friends from junior high went to another high school and though it wasn't their fault, I felt they betrayed me. I felt hurt. Then Brian came along and he thought I was cool. He was nineteen—I think he had repeated a couple grades; I can't remember. At first he was really nice to me and it felt great. But then he got mean. I tried to dump him but I was afraid to, not because I thought he'd get meaner, but because I was afraid that I would be back where I was—alone, uncool, and stupid. That's when I started drinking. He had some friends who partied on the weekends and he asked me to join him.

"His friends thought I was too straight so I began dressing like them. You know, my parents never said anything to me about the way I was dressing. That's odd, don't you think? I mean, if my kid went from wearing ordinary decent clothes that were kind of pretty to wearing dingy black pants and lace shirts, I'd say something!"

Actually her mother had said something; she had challenged Lori on her dress, her grades, her behavior, and Lori had exploded: slammed doors, screamed "I hate you!" and all the rest. I didn't remind her of that; kids can have conveniently forgetful memories.

"Yeah, I just spiraled out of control," she continued. "Drinking, weed, bad grades, and then I got kicked out of school. That's when I decided it was time to run. I had no idea where I was going to go, but I just knew I had to leave. I had to get out, get away from something, even if I didn't know what it was. That's when I decided that it was my dad. He was what I needed to leave. He had never really been there for me, you know? He worked all the time and I remember my mom complaining. He was a great guy, but, you know, I never knew him super well. Not like I do now."

"Besides working hard, your dad hadn't done anything to drive you away, had he?"

"I'm not really sure," she said, after a long, awkward pause. Then she said something that every father should hear. She said, *"I just picked him to be mad at."*

The fifteen-year-old Lori wasn't mad at her father; he took the fall because he was the safe guy, the steady one, the one who would never leave *her*, even if she left *him*. Daughters crave the support and loyalty of their fathers—and often test them to prove it.

"That's when we all sat together in your office. Do you remember, Dr. Meeker?"

Sure I remembered; I remembered sitting next to the door, blocking it, which was my usual strategy when angry kids were in the room.

"I'll never forget you telling my dad that he should take me canoeing. 'What a dumb thing to say,' I thought. Do you realize that you made me madder at my dad?" Of course I knew that, but that wasn't the point; the point was that she needed help from the person she secretly loved most—her father.

"The next week at our house was miserable. Here was my poor dad, an indoor guy who liked to watch football on the weekends, figuring out how to take me canoeing down the Pine. I watched him put our gear together and I hated thinking about what the trip would be like. But I knew in my heart that part of me really wanted to be alone with him, alone with my dad. But I never told him. I could barely confess that to myself."

"Does he know that now?"

"No. But it's true. Somewhere deep inside me I had this feeling that I needed to be alone with my dad. It was just there."

I understood.

"Anyway, finally we left. My mom and little sister stayed at home and my dad loaded our car. Bless his heart. I don't think he had any idea what he was doing! Our equipment was borrowed and he was probably more nervous than I was.

"The first day was miserable. It was hot, the bugs were everywhere, and I was being eaten alive. I tried to paddle faster to get away from them. My dad always paddled from the back and I was glad because I couldn't see him. I didn't want to talk and I certainly didn't want a lecture from him. That would have been the worst: if he had asked me a million questions or told me how bad Brian was for me or how bad I was for being kicked out of school.

"And do you know what was amazing, Dr. Meeker? He never asked me one question that day. He and I just paddled. I remember sitting in the front feeling so angry and frustrated that I wanted to scream, over and over, but I didn't. And my dad didn't even do anything to make me scream! I guess I was kind of hoping that he would say something that would irritate me so that I would have an excuse to let it rip!

"Then we set camp for the night and my dad made us mac and cheese in a pot. I told him it was terrible. But actually it tasted really good. That was the first time I remember feeling my anger quiet down just a bit. I guess the mac and cheese did it. We ate in silence. He would look at me with this sad face and I felt bad. I knew my dad was hurting but even that made me mad.

"The next day we packed up, and down the river we went. The second day was weirder than the first. I started irritating my dad. I'd yell something at him like 'What's wrong with you, you're steering us into the trees' or 'I can't believe that you never want to be home; you make mom cry you know!' Just random things. Nothing made sense. I was just trying to get under his skin. I think I really wanted him to yell at me so that I would have a real reason to be mad! How crazy is that?"

Lori sat a moment and shook her head. She seemed amazed at her ridiculous behavior. I said, "You were a fifteen-year-old kid who disliked herself. Life is hard for kids. In many ways you were doing the best you could." I wasn't trying to let her off the hook; I was trying to help her figure out what had happened. The more we talked, the more pensive she became.

"I was mean, just mean," she said. "But dad just stayed quiet and didn't take the bait. I don't know that I could have done that. I would have bitten my head off. The day seemed long. Kind of funny how being angry makes life feel like it's dragging on. He even made mac and cheese the second night. I don't think he thought about food much. He just wasn't an outdoor guy.

"The third day, something broke loose in me. I cried and cried. And I had no idea what I was crying about. This made my dad really uncomfortable! Poor guy. He had no idea what he was sign-ing up for when he agreed to that trip. Neither of us had. I see now that that's one of the cool things about going off on an adventure, even if it's not under the best circumstances. You never know what's going to happen. We sure didn't.

"Dad just kept paddling. I cried; he paddled. I think the harder I cried, the faster he paddled. I didn't know why I was so sad and I know he didn't have a clue but here's the strange and wonderful thing. He didn't seem to need to know. If my mom had been there, she would have pummeled me with questions. That's just her per-sonality."

Frankly, it is mine too. If she had been my daughter, I would have pummeled her with questions. I think most mothers would do the same. But dads are different, and sometimes that quiet strength is just what a daughter needs.

"I can't remember what we ate that night," she continued, "but it doesn't matter. What happened the next day was a miracle. We talked to each other. No yelling; just some tears and then quiet paddling. Then we'd talk again. I think that was the first time that my dad really heard me and I heard him. Before the trip we were two people who loved and respected each other living in the same house. We had cordial conversations about grades, what I liked to do or how my day was but that was about it. But that day, the fourth day of our trip, we talked to each other and it felt so good.

"My dad said he was sorry that I was so angry. He didn't ask why I was mad and that's a good thing because I wouldn't have known what to tell him. Then he said that he was *glad to be with me on the river that day.* Can you imagine? He said that he was actually happy to be with me—this nasty kid with gnarly hair and military boots—on this river. When he said it, something deep inside of me welled up. It wasn't nerves. It was a calm, deep knowledge that this man loved me. I was overcome with emotion. Of course I began to cry again.

"By the end of our trip, neither of us was ready to go home. We didn't say so, but we knew how the other felt. There was regret that we didn't have more time to paddle and talk, to watch for egrets and eagles. I felt desperate to stay on the river because that was the first time that I had ever felt content. And the first time that I had felt my dad's love. Until then, I knew that he loved me because I figured he had to—he was my dad. It was just something that was—like my dog always being there when I came home from school. I didn't pay attention to my dad's feelings for me and I'm not sure he did either but when we were on the river, those feelings smacked me between my eyes. They were unavoidable."

Lori's eyes welled with tears and she smiled. Then she said something extraordinary. "Dr. Meeker, do you think that I'll ever be able to find a husband who will love my kids that well?"

You could say that those four days spent camping with her dad changed her life—and they did. But it was also the culmination of everything her father had done for her all through her life, things she never fully appreciated until then. From his patience, forgiveness, love, and commitment she gained emotional stability when she needed it most.

Many good dads focus naturally on the exterior—on their children's academic performance or artistic excellence in drawing or playing the piano or their skill at sports. These are all good things, but far more important is the interior life of the child, which entails character, emotion, and spirit. And here's a secret: your kids *want you to be part of that interior world*. They *know* that it's more important than all the external things, and they want you to recognize it and help them with it.

They need you to answer three critical questions.

Question 1:
Dad, How Do You Really Feel about Me?

When you hold your newborn son, he feels safe. When you hum a tune at bedtime he feels content. Throughout his early life he needs to know that you love him. Yes, young children are more strongly attached to their mothers than their fathers, but that's just a developmental stage. In the long term, no one can take your place in your son's imagination or your daughter's heart.

When children hit pre-puberty, their attention often turns from their mother to their father, with boys needing to learn what it is to be a man and girls needing to know what they should expect from a man. Boys need a father's affirmation of their masculinity; girls need their fathers to confirm that they are loved and valued. The trick for dads is to never assume that your children know that they are loved and valued. Communicating your love for your child is so extremely important.

Lori's father had provided for her exterior world by working hard so that the family could afford a middle-class life. But when Lori didn't feel pretty, smart, athletic, or good at much, when her exterior world failed to deliver, she hit a crisis. She needed her father to reaffirm that those external things were far less important than the fact that he cared about her. When Lori asked me, "Will I be able to find a husband who will love my kids that well?" I knew her father had nailed it—he had proved that he loved her, which was more important than anything else.

Many fathers worry about communicating their feelings to their daughters. Don't worry. Daughters—and sons—are forgiving of your awkwardness, even of past disagreements, and they want your love. How would you respond if your father knocked on your door and said, "Son, will you let me come in? There's something very important I need to tell you." Even if your relationship had been bad, you'd almost certainly hear him out; and unconsciously, you would almost certainly still want his approval and respect.

When a daughter grows up knowing that her dad loves her, she's going places in life, because she knows she is valuable, significant, worth loving, and worth fighting for; and with boys it is much the same. Teach him that he is loved and he will grow into a man with self-confidence, who can make his way in the world and love others.

Here are some ways that you can begin to answer this critical question for your son or daughter.

1. Show up. Not just at key events, but every day; and be fully present. When your son asks you a question, put down your phone, sit in front of him, and make eye contact. *That's* showing up, *that's* being fully present.

When your daughter comes home from a date, meet her at the door and give her a hug. Invite her to the kitchen for a cookie or a glass of water and give her a chance to talk, if she wants. She may turn you down, she may even accuse you of spying on her, but in reality, she'll know you care; she'll know you love her.

No, you don't need to be at every ballgame, practice, or recital. In fact, it's more important to be there day to day, for all the mundane things—whether it's homework, or driving the kids to school, or working side by side with them doing yardwork. The more you are an engaged part of their everyday lives, the better, because that's when magic happens. It's partly a cumulative effect; it's partly that you never know when a child will suddenly say, "Dad, tell me about...."

2. Say something. Many men are hesitant to say "I love you"—often because their own fathers never said it to them. But you need to get those words out, even if you have to practice them in front of a mirror before you address your seventeen-year-old son. Do it. The impact will be enormous.

Timing is important too. You don't want your love to be conditional on success—like getting a good grade or winning a game. It's more important to say it when your daughter strikes out with the bases loaded or fails an exam or is crying over a broken-off relationship with a boyfriend. Kids need your strength when they are weak.

3. Never shy away. All children try to push their parents away from them. A two-year-old will stomp her feet and call you a bad daddy. A six-year-old will slam his math book shut when you try to help him. A thirteen-year-old might make a nasty face and try to dodge a hug. *Never, ever, take it personally.* Their behavior is not about you, it's about them. When children feel insecure, out of control, or self-conscious they can get snarky.

One of the most powerful ways to prove your love is to stay put and stay engaged. Keep paddling the canoe. The calmer you stay, the quicker your child will calm down too.

Question 2:
Dad, What Do You Believe about Me?

Unless you *tell* your children what you believe about them— what you think their talents are, what their character is like, what you expect of them—you might be surprised what *they* think.

I was giving Quinn a check-up for kindergarten. He said his dad was overseas fighting in a war and that he missed him terribly, and couldn't wait for him to come home. He was proud of his dad and tried to describe his uniform for me.

"My dad really misses me," he said. "He's proud of me and says I need to be the man of the house while he's gone. My mom says I don't, but I believe my dad. He's tough, you know, and when he comes home he's gonna take me hunting. But I have to be twelve to shoot a gun, he says, because I'm too young now." Quinn talked rapidly and his voice seemed strained.

"Yup. My dad told me that I'm the smartest kid he's ever known. He's right, you know. I am smart. I read every day because I know that when my dad gets home he's going to want me to read with him."

I asked Quinn to get a book from the waiting room to show me how well he could read. When he stepped out, I asked his mother about his dad. "He's in jail," she started. Then she broke down crying. "He never calls. He doesn't write either. He got busted for drunk driving and was so humiliated he couldn't bear to tell Quinn where he went. We told him that dad had work to do far away.

Quinn turned that into he was overseas fighting a war. I just didn't have the heart to correct him."

Children have vivid imaginations and at six, which was Quinn's age, it's not unusual for them to create an imaginary friend. In Quinn's case he was creating an imaginary father to make up for the absence of a real one. It was okay for the moment, but eventually he would, gently, have to be told the truth. Neither his mom nor I looked forward to that moment.

Quinn imagined what his father believed about him—and maybe he was right, maybe his father did think he was the smartest boy on the planet; maybe he had told Quinn so earlier. The important thing was that Quinn was sustained by his belief that his father was proud of him, and believed him to be strong and smart.

Quinn's father was set to be released from jail in the next few months. My hope was that he would reaffirm his son's faith in what his dad believed about him. That would make the transition much easier.

The academic research has shown us that kids who have good communication with their fathers are much less likely to have trouble with drugs, alcohol, or depression.[1] It seems as though dads have a unique power to boost their children's sense of self-worth, of being grounded, and of belonging, which acts as a shield not just against drugs, alcohol, and depression, but also (and what is often related) teenage sexual activity.

Whether your son or daughter is three years old or forty-three years old the need for dad's affirmation is always there. They are your children forever, and they will always need to know what dad believes about them.

Here's how you can help fill that need.

1) **Communicate simple truth.** Kids see right through platitudes and hype. It's no good getting C's in school and having your father boast that you are one of the smartest kids in the class, if you still can't get your grades up, no matter how much you apply yourself. So praise needs to be honest. If your child is getting C's and that's the best he can do, tell him that's fine, that you admire his tenacity for working so hard, and help him discover the subjects or practical skills at which he can excel, while he hammers out his C's in Calculus or English.

As a parent you should be positive—and *never* talk critically of your children to other people—but you also want to be truthful. Your kids will appreciate that—and appreciate that C's in math don't spell the end of your affection for them or mean that they're mediocre in everything, or for that matter that with enough effort and time they can't improve in math!

2) **Praise their character, not the stuff they do.** Kids want to know what you think they're made of deep down. So tell them, "I believe that you are courageous, strong, patient, committed, hardworking, chivalrous," or whatever the case may be.

3) **Let them catch you talking about them.** When I was rejected from every medical school I applied to at twenty-one, I thought my life was over. I thought I was too stupid to go and that's why I was rejected. One day I overheard my father talking on the phone to a friend and telling him that I would be going to medical school in the very near future. I was stunned. In that moment, my life changed. I was filled with the deep knowledge that my dad believed I could succeed in medical school. That was it. I was going. Period. That overheard conversation meant nothing to my father; it meant everything to me.

When you really believe in your kids, they'll hear it in your voice. If they hear you talking about your belief in their goodness, perseverance, or courage, they will believe it—and it might just change their lives.

4) Take advantage of their failure. The very best time to communicate sincere belief in your son or daughter is during a time when they feel they have failed. Then, their self-esteem is low, they are thinking that they are worthless, dumb, incapable. That is the perfect time for you to step in with a smile and say, "I don't care what just happened on the field, I don't care that you just flunked your exam, I know what you are made of and I believe in you. So stand up again and get back at it." These are words that change your kids' lives.

Question 3:
Dad, What Are Your Hopes for Me?

One of my favorite things to do is walk into an auditorium filled with high schoolers and talk to them about sex. Believe it or not, it's fun—primarily because they really want to hear what I have to say. No one talks to them about a subject that is on their minds constantly. So when I speak, I have a very attentive audience.

Here is one thing that I have learned about kids over the years: children under thirteen don't think beyond a week and teens don't think much beyond a year or two. Teens believe that the best times of their lives are in the *immediate* future and that when they're adults life will get boring. I try to give them a bigger perspective. I tell teens that they have to be very careful about what they do sexually at seventeen because their bodies are created for at least fifty years' worth of sex. That gets their attention!

Your son or daughter lives for today, with maybe a few worries about tomorrow. Much of this thinking is developmentally appropriate and can be hard to shift. If you have a child who struggles with anxiety, low self-esteem, or depression, he will be more prone to believing that life is short because he can't imagine life getting any better. And for some kids, the truth is, life may be shorter.

Several years ago I went to address junior high students in an underprivileged neighborhood near Los Angeles. Many of the boys were in gangs, and a few weeks before I arrived, two boys had died in a neighborhood shooting.

The teacher introduced me and mentioned a few of the shows I'd done and books I'd written, and these kids were entirely unimpressed. That's what I love about kids. They don't care about where you've been or what you've accomplished, they want to know one thing: Do you like them or not? I began talking about sex, the good parts, the riskiness of it, and I talked about their feelings. As I worked to encourage them to hold off on sex until they were older, I realized that I had to define older. At one time, when Julie Gerberding, M.D., was head of the Centers for Disease Control and Prevention (2002–2008), she wrote about driving down rates of cervical cancer. She said that the best way to reduce the risk of getting cervical cancer was to decrease the number of sexual partners to as few as possible and delay sexual activity for as long as possible (or until marriage).[2] (The reason for delaying the sexual debut is because we know that girls who start having sex when they are older than sixteen, have fewer lifetime sexual partners.)[3] The girls— and the boys—seated in front of me needed to know this.

We started talking and the kids opened up. Many of them, even though they were only twelve or thirteen, were sexually experienced. Boys boasted about the girls they had "gotten" and the girls got mad because they (who had been "gotten") felt the boys didn't really care about them but only about "scoring." Many of the girls swore that they would never have sex again, because they felt that they had been used, and I had just told them how dangerous that could be.

But the idea of postponing sex until marriage was completely foreign to most of them, because most of their parents weren't married. Many of them also fatalistically assumed that they weren't going to live past twenty-five anyway, so they had to experience as much of life as possible before then. This broke my heart. My job then became one of teaching them about their futures. It shifted from talking about delaying sex and reducing sexual partners to a much harder conversation about how they could find a better future.

Your daughter might not be attending a school with high-risk students, but she does have one thing in common with them: she isn't thinking much about life after twenty-one. Marriage, kids, careers can all seem like very distant prospects when you're a teen, more like dreams than an approaching reality. Too often teens think solely about present gratification without regard to later consequences. Your job is to shift their perspective, to help them understand that delaying gratification now is part of having a much better, and longer-lasting, future later with even greater rewards (a happy marriage is far more gratifying than a—physically and mentally risky—one-night stand).

Now we must address a sensitive subject: divorce. If you are a divorced man, you need to understand that the idea of marriage may not sit well with your son or daughter. Children of divorced parents often feel a sense of abandonment, anger at both parents, and anger at themselves. They also often have a fear of marriage, and don't see it in their future. Divorce can actually perpetuate itself in lower rates of marriage and more fragile relationships.

I tell you this, if you're a divorced father, so that you can help your children. What you *don't* need to do is to discuss your marital failures or mistakes so that your children can avoid the same ones, because often that discussion has the opposite effect. The very fact that you did something validates it in your child's mind. So if you had an affair, having an affair doesn't seem that bad, or, they might think, it's something to be expected. If you had a drinking problem, they might decide that drinking is an acceptable way to deal with a problem. And so on.

After a conference, a man asked me how he should tell his seven-year-old son about his past. The man had recently been released from prison on drug possession and trafficking charges. While he was in prison, his wife divorced him and won custody of the child. She had also posted on her refrigerator an 8 x 11 photograph of him in his orange prison jumpsuit to remind their son "never to do what his dad did." Dad hated the idea of that photo almost as much as he hated the idea of his son following his footsteps. What was he to do?

"The minute you leave this conference," I said, "I want you to go to your ex-wife's home and take that picture down. Burn it. The photo brings nothing but shame to you and to your son. Shame never motivates children (or adults) to change their ways. When your seven-year-old son sees that photo, he sees his hero with an orange jumpsuit on. He doesn't see a criminal or a man who made mistakes. He sees his dad—and if dad was in prison, that's good enough for him, and he might end up there too, just to prove that he was just as bad. That's how a child thinks. A far better way to put him on the right path is to be there for him, and live up to the hero image he has of you."

Because I was angry at what his ex-wife had done, I probably said more than I should have. "You are done with prison. Finished.

It is behind you. You need to believe that and live that and communicate it to your son. The best thing that you can do is to commit to living an honorable life before his very eyes. To keep him from a wrong turn, show him a better way. He wants to be like you, so be the man you want *him* to be."

That advice is true for *every* dad.

In my work with the NFL I have talked to men about why some abused their girlfriends. I asked one such man how his colleagues had the self-control to play an elite sport but couldn't control their tempers at home. His answer was startling.

"For many boys who grow up in poverty without a father, violence is part of our lives. We see hitting and hear screaming. Often, as kids, we're the victims. We don't see fathers and mothers; we don't even see boyfriends and girlfriends; we just see single abandoned moms. There is no excuse for what men do, but it's true that growing up that way you don't learn how to treat a girlfriend or a wife; and a lot of us grew up with a lot of anger, because we resented not having a dad around to protect us and our mom.

"And think about it. We get paid millions of dollars to be as aggressive as possible on the field. To live right on that edge of explosion without crossing the line. Then we go home and we're supposed to know how to turn that aggression off; many guys, especially from backgrounds like mine, don't know how." I asked him whether the sexual promiscuity of some players was part and parcel of the same thing.

"Yeah, you know, they got the money, the fame, the power, and there are a lot of women who want a part of that."

"And the guys do it for the gratification, or the power, or just because they can?"

"Sure, there's that, but they also think that's what their fathers did. If he wasn't dead or in prison they assume their dad was sleeping around because they sure never saw him. That's the role model they've got."

Many of the very same NFL players who revel in stories of their greatest plays or victories have also told me how between plays their eyes almost involuntarily drift to the stands to see if their dad is there, *even if they haven't seen their dad for years.* That's the sort of impact dads have. Even when you're not around, your children are wondering about you, imagining how you behave, looking for you, trying to emulate you, and yearning to win your approval.

Sons often choose their careers paths in order to impress their fathers. Daughters often marry men who in some way resemble their fathers (so be careful how you behave). For the rest of their lives you will be an inescapable part of them. That's a heavy responsibility—and it is rightly yours. It is what being a father means. So take the opportunity now to make your presence a good one. Let's look specifically at ways you can give your son or daughter hope for the future.

1) Talk about their futures in specific ways. Talk about what they might be doing, where they might be living, whether they might be married or a parent at twenty-five, thirty-five, or even forty-five. For most kids, that's a mind-bending exercise (in a good way). It's also a way to get them thinking about their calling in life, setting priorities for their future, and understanding that their future is even more important than their present—and that you care about the choices they make.

2) Dream with them. Most of us naturally want our kids or grandkids to live out our dreams, but we need to let them have their own dreams, *and dream with them.* You can do that by asking open-ended questions. "You seem to like reading history books? Who do you like reading about most?" or "I notice you get excited when we talk baseball. Is baseball your favorite sport?" Not all the conversations should be career-related or about what they already do in school or on the playing field. You can ask about things that make them happy or content. Or you can point out things in their character—tenacity, humility, kindness—that will stand them in good stead in the future. Use the conversations to bring your children's dreams—their projected futures—to life. And teens and young adults who think about their futures have a better sense of perspective and are less inclined to endanger their future with bad behavior. A sense of perspective is one of the best gifts you can bestow on a teen.

Being a dad is not about passing on a huge inheritance, connections for a great job, a down payment on a first house, or even paying for the best college.

Think about what you wanted from your dad. What you probably wanted most was to know what he thought about you. Did he believe in your ability to be a good man, to live an honorable life? Or did he doubt you and make you think you were never good enough? (And if so, how much would you pay now to hear him say he really didn't mean it?) Did your dad love you the way you needed him to love you? You can answer that question right now, and if he didn't, then you need to do better with your own children.

Your children look up to you, and you can change their lives in the profoundest of ways. They trust you; they need you to be there for them; they crave your approval.

Being a great dad is really quite simple. Don't worry about your mistakes, because they are far less important than your successes.

And to be a success all you need to answer are three questions. That's it. They are the starting place—and in many ways the ending place—of being a really good father. So get to it.

CHAPTER 6

Focus On the Play, Not the Game

A s a woman who was pregnant five times, I can tell you that pregnant women don't feel terrific, and I know that can color a man's ideas about the "joys" of pregnancy and being a father. I know I was often irritable, depressed, tearful, nauseated, and angry, and I even passed out a few times. I occasionally blamed my husband for my condition, and given that I was exhausted and had trouble even putting my socks on, you can imagine how attractive the idea of sex was. The answer is, it was not. All this is to say, gentlemen, that if being a father frightens you, you're in good company. Being a mother frightens your wife just as much.

But both of you need to stay the course, because all that suffering is well worth it—in fact, it brings the greatest joy you can have in life, which is a family; and every stage along the way has its rewards. The cute baby and kid stages might be obvious. But there's also the flattery of seeing your son in his twenties get married to someone just like your wife, because he saw what a good example the both of you were, or maybe he's serving in the Navy like you did, or maybe your daughter is following in your footsteps to become a doctor (as I did).

So here's some advice—no matter how frightened you are at the thought of becoming a father or how difficult you find it being a father—you should never get discouraged. Your wife might be giving you a hard time or your kids might be defiant; it doesn't matter. You are the center of their lives, and no matter how much they might complain, they're depending on you. They need someone strong to lean on. They need someone with determination and perseverance when times are hard. They need someone who is a practical problem solver. Your wife needs you as a husband; your kids need you as a dad. In fact, your kids need both of you: mom for understanding, dad for fixing stuff—and not just mechanical stuff, *but everything*. You might find your complementary approaches to problems frustrating, but your kids need both. Moms usually want to find out how a problem started and get to grips with all the nuances of an issue. Dads want to cut to a solution. Or in football terms, women want to talk about the game, dads want to run the play.

That metaphor isn't mine. I got it from my friend Benjamin Watson, who plays tight end for the Baltimore Ravens. Truth be told, I don't even know what a tight end is, but I do know some very important things about Benjamin. He is a great father and husband. He once told me, "You know, Meg, being a good dad is a lot like being a good football player. Coaches tell us that when we focus on the plays not the game, we're more likely to win the game. For dads, that approach really works. Focus on what's in front of you; focus on the task at hand; and the big picture will take care of itself. Focus on the play."

Bingo. When it comes to being a great dad, there are six key plays that you can practice that will help you win the game of raising happy, successful children and will keep you a hero in your son's or daughter's eyes.

Play #1
Play with Your Kids

Timothy's dad was a small town doctor who worked long hours. Timothy didn't have the chance to see his father as much as he wanted, but when I spoke with Timothy, who was then in high school, about his father, he didn't seem bitter or resentful. In fact, he adored his dad and said that he wanted to be a physician, too, when he grew up.

Timothy told me, "I know people think that my father should have been home more and I heard my mom complain a lot. But here's the thing. When I was with my dad, we had a lot of fun together.

"When I was in elementary school, I remember getting up at night and sneaking downstairs because I could smell my dad's cigar smoke coming from the patio. I'd go sit with him, and we'd talk, and he taught me all the constellations. I loved those nights because it was just me and my dad, all alone.

"My mom got mad at my dad for letting me stay up with him. For a while I stopped, but then my dad winked at me, and sitting outside at night became our secret. We did it for years.

"We'd see who could find the most constellations the fastest. Once we did, we had to say their names and how many stars were in them. The coolest thing was that sometimes he let me win and other times he didn't. I loved that he didn't always let me win because it made me feel that he respected me."

Several years after our conversation Timothy indeed went to medical school and I can't help but believe that those nights on the patio played an enormous part in his decision.

Studies show that boys are much more likely to grow up to be like their fathers if they had a close and warm relationship with them. That stands to figure, doesn't it? For most kids that warmth and closeness comes from playing with dad. The fact that dads are playful can sometimes drive mothers crazy. But playing with dad can give kids the self-confidence to challenge themselves and take healthy risks—and that's important for character development.

Interestingly, it's been shown that when mothers teach their kids to swim, they usually stand in front of them so that they can make eye contact and encourage their children forward to the safety of their arms. When fathers did the teaching, they stood behind their children so that the kids faced not a sympathetic pair of encouraging eyes, but the challenge of the water. One way of teaching is not necessarily better than the other, but it is certainly interesting the different messages that are sent. Moms communicate to kids, "You need me to help you and here I am"; dads communicate, "You face the water and swim; I know you can do it."

But maybe even more important, dads are far more likely to *play* with their children in the water than moms are. How important is that? More important than you might think, according to Paul Raeburn, author of *Do Fathers Matter? What Science Is Telling Us About the Parent We've Overlooked*. Here are some great statistics he illuminates in his book on the benefits of fathers playing with their children.

- A child's language development soars when his father talks to him during play
- If a father reads picture books to his child (starting at age six months), her expressiveness at fifteen months will be significantly better and her language skills, when she's three years old will be much more advanced
- When a father plays affectionately with a child, the child gets along better with peers later in life
- When fathers play active games with their children, they encourage them to be brave and take more risks
- A child's need to play and be stimulated, pushed, and encouraged is as important as his need for stability and security
- Children had significantly fewer behavior problems, delinquency, or criminal behavior as adolescents when their fathers engaged in play, read to them, and took them on outings

That's from the research, but I can also tell you from observation that toddlers will instinctively reach for their fathers when they are happy because they know their father will throw them up into the air, tickle their bellies, or wrestle with them on the ground. Kids love the physical contact, affection, and levity of play with their fathers.

If you want to raise self-assured, confident kids, *play with them*. Nothing diffuses tension for kids or fathers like going on a bike ride, playing catch, running around, or going for a swim.

When a toddler throws tantrums, a child refuses to work harder at school, or a teen starts drifting from you, amp up your playtime. It's something of a cure-all when kids start acting up. Play will get you closer to your child, no matter what his age.

Play #2
Pray with Your Kids

One of the fundamental rules of raising great kids is to understand and accept one truth: God is good for kids. Whether you are religious or not, children are more God-minded than most adults, and take security from the idea of a divinely ordered world. You might scoff—the parents of the kids in question often do—but many children have told me about seeing angels and what the angels have told them. Whether we want to believe these kids or not, it is undeniable that children tend to be very spiritually minded, and as a father you need to be ready to answer spiritual questions.

In their book, *Born to Believe*, Dr. Robert Newberg and Mark Robert Waldman describe how all children are born with an intuitive faith in God, or, if you prefer, knowledge of the unseen. Children are hard-wired for faith, which is why praying with your children is so important. Praying with your child satisfies her need to connect with God. Kids like prayer. When you pray with them, it gives them security. It reminds them that even when you're not there, God is watching over them. And prayer will draw you closer to your children. Prayer is an intimate act. It is something you do together that seems profoundly important. And it underlines for your children that even their big, strong, hero dad gets down on his knees to acknowledge and seek guidance from the God who gives us our moral law to live by.

If you ever prayed with your father, as I did, you know what I mean. Having a strong, powerful, smart dad kneel by your bedside, close his eyes, and pray brings a child closer to his father than any activity or conversation ever can. Many fathers feel uncomfortable praying with their kids because they don't know what to say and they fear looking silly. Your kids look at it completely differently—they see a hero who shares their instinctive faith. They are less focused on the words you say, than on the very fact that you are kneeling and acknowledging the power of God, which your children feel intuitively.

Gillian remembers bedtime prayers with her father like they happened two years ago. In fact, they occurred more than forty years ago but she still tears up when she talks about them.

"As an adult, I can honestly say that the image of my dad at my bedside or holding my hands when he sat in his reading chair and prayed for me changed me. I don't remember what he said and it didn't really matter. I heard him ask God to help me and I felt so loved. I knew when he asked God that he really saw what I was going through. He sometimes cried when he prayed and that made my heart melt. His example of prayerful strength touched me then, and it guided me later in life, when I had a family of my own."

Prayer changes people. It changed me with some of the most precious and profound experiences I've ever had.

My father died of Alzheimer's disease several years ago. During the last months of his life, he had difficulty speaking, and I couldn't even tell whether he knew who I was. But there was one thing he never forgot—and that was how to pray. When we prayed, he bowed his head and closed his eyes. That reaction—when almost every other memory he had was gone—proved to me that God was present with my father.

Shortly before he died, I grabbed his hands and began praying the Lord's Prayer. "Our Father, who art in heaven, hallowed be thy name. Thy kingdom come, thy will be done on earth as it is in heaven." I felt his hands tremble a bit. I looked at him and saw tears streaming down his face. In that moment, I felt that God was with my father; I didn't want that moment to end. Not only did my father know we were praying, but he knew who God was. When every other memory failed him, knowledge of God did not, and it brought us together in a way that I cannot adequately explain, except that I feel it still.

As a parent, as a prayerful parent, you can give your son or daughter experiences that transcend your own understanding. Sit beside your child, close your eyes, and open yourself up to the living God that your son or daughter probably already knows and already believes in. They want you to be a part of that. Nothing will bring your family closer together in a truly meaningful way than daily family prayer.

Play #3
Be Steady

Children need you to be calm when they are agitated, strong when they are weak, confident when they are fearful. That, in many ways, is what being a dad is all about. When kids are acting up, a strong, quiet dad is usually much more capable of dealing with the problem than emotion-laden mom—and I say that as a mother *and* as a pediatrician. Women have more hormonal fluctuations than men do; they are also more likely to take things personally; and they are more easily driven to emotional reactions.

So be steady. Strive always to be the voice of reason, courage, and faith. It's what kids expect of their heroes. It's what they, and your wife, expect of *you*.

When kids act up, mothers want to understand why; and while emotional understanding and sympathy are wonderful things, so is the man, the dad, who approaches every issue in a straightforward, dependable way, who cuts through emotional fog with calm, steady, trustworthy reason.

Yes, men often have tempers. We all know that. But the flip side is that for most men those tempers flare only occasionally. Far more often, as I've seen working with parents and their kids, men can be extraordinarily calm and focused during a crisis.

If you want a football analogy, it's like a quarterback leading a team down the field with less than two minutes to go in the game. Men have an ability to execute their roles coolly under pressure; quarterbacks, or most successful leaders for that matter, have the ability to lead with a steady, calm demeanor. That's what people respond to, and that's a role model for a dad: be steady, be dependable, be focused.

Play #4
Be Honest

Honesty is enormously important for children—and if you want your children's trust, you need to be honest with them.

I know that being honest can be hard, and many of us assume that indulging a small, white lie can be an act of kindness. But children never like being lied to, even if the lies seem trivial to parents. Children instinctively believe, as Albert Einstein did, that "Anyone who doesn't take truth seriously in small matters cannot be trusted in large ones either." Nothing more endangers the trust your child places in you than dishonesty. When you tell the truth, on the other hand, you teach that reality is nothing to fear. When they see you telling the truth, they see bravery and they learn that they, too, can confront any situation. But when they hear lies, they intuit that you don't believe that they have what it takes to handle the truth, and they, as a consequence, become more fearful and insecure. Trust, integrity, and truth are all part of being a hero, and all part of being a dad. Be the man of integrity, be the man they can trust, be the man who tells the truth.

Suni had been my patient since she was five, and during all that time it was quite clear to me that she adored her father, but now that she was about to go off to college, something was wrong. I tried to talk to her about the usual college perils of sex, drinking, and drugs, but she kept talking compulsively about her father, talking about all the wonderful times they had had together—until now.

"Suni, what happened?"

"All those years we played at the playground, all those years we had dad-daughter dates, he was cheating on us. I mean, all this time, I guess—I still can't fully believe it; I'm not really sure—my dad had a girlfriend. He betrayed us all—my mom, my brother—everyone."

"When did you find this out?"

"A couple of months ago; a friend of my mom's saw him playing golf with another woman. She followed them for a while around the golf course and realized that they weren't just friends. She told my mother and then my mother asked my dad if it was true.

"They've always had problems, my mom and dad, but I never thought that my dad would do anything like that. I just feel so confused. Was my life a lie? Did my dad ever love me? I mean—all those nights we spent playing, going to movies—was he faking it? Mom and dad are trying to work it out, but I don't know what's true and what's not true anymore."

Suni learned later that her father's affair had been going on for several months. Fortunately, he dropped the girlfriend and worked hard to make amends with his family. But he had a hard road ahead of him. His children distrusted his affection for them. They doubted his sincerity. More than that, they now questioned *everything* they ever thought about their father before, which is a common reaction.

Let me put your son's and daughter's needs very simply. If you want to remain a hero, tell the truth; and even better than that, live the truth.

Play #5
Be Firm

It might be unfashionable, Dad, but you need to be a good disciplinarian. Many parents today want to be their children's "friends." Get this loud and clear, you are not their friend. You are their dad. I'll be completely honest here: my husband was the primary disciplinarian in our home because I hate conflict, and many mothers have a hard time with discipline because their feelings get in the way. But discipline is still necessary, and, Dad, you need to step up to be the enforcer of the family rules.

Now let me be clear: being a firm disciplinarian has *nothing* to do with being harsh or critical or angry or cruel or mean or hurtful or yelling or dredging up past offenses or inflicting unreasonable punishments. That's *bad* discipline. Good discipline has everything to do with:

- You being in charge (of your child and yourself)
- Self-restraint and calm that leads to measured, reasoned responses
- Yes meaning yes, and no meaning no
- Setting clear, consistent standards of behavior, with boundaries that expand as your child grows older

When you need to be a disciplinarian, give yourself time (it can be minutes or hours)—and time away from the child in question—to decide what discipline is necessary and appropriate. The goal is tough love—*for your child's benefit*—not retaliation. The benefits of good discipline are:

- Stronger, less self-indulgent, more self-reliant kids
- Kids with better self-control, which will help them in all aspects of their lives
- Kids who feel loved, because you care about what they do and how they behave

Many years ago, a researcher conducted a study on men in their twenties who were incarcerated. He wanted to find out what, if anything, these jailed men had in common.

His discovery: every man lamented that when he was growing up, "no one cared enough to say no." That was it—not race, not socio-economic status, not how much education they had. What united every prisoner was a lack of discipline in his early life, because no one cared enough to say no. You need to care enough to be the disciplinarian.

Daniel was a divorced, single dad to three girls, ages four, seven, and nine years old, of whom he had partial custody. The girls alternated between living with him for a week and living with their mom for a week. Not knowing what to do, not knowing how to be a good father to his three young daughters in this stressful situation, he studied his girls, listened to them intently, and he talked to their teachers. He liked playing with them—that was easy. But setting rules? That seemed a lot harder, especially given that he would likely have different rules than his wife. I told him to follow his instincts. He wanted guidelines, so I gave him these:

1. Dad is in charge—no debates over authority in his house (but be patient, ask questions, and listen when they talk).
2. No fights over food—they eat what you eat, though maybe with a dash of color.
3. No fights over hairstyle or clothes—go shopping with them and buy clothes that guard their modesty.
4. No being bored—do fun things on the weekends.
5. Make sure they have a bedtime/curfew when they get older.

His job was to set good rules and make them stick, be patient, keep talking (and listening) to his daughters, and not to worry about what his wife did or what other parents did with their kids.

The girls' mother wanted them to "like being with her," so she let them do whatever they wanted. She gave them cell phones when they were seven. She never made them go to bed at a reasonable time. Often she let the girls sleep in her bed. If the girls wanted three different things for dinner, she cooked what each of the daughters wanted.

All this put Daniel in a tough situation. When the girls turned up at his doorstep, they were in a sour mood. "They wouldn't talk much—except to throw fits over homework and bedtimes; otherwise I got one-word answers." Over and over they told him "You're mean! Mom never makes us do this!" to the point where he *almost* responded, "Well, then go back to your mother's if you like her so much!" Of course, he didn't. He bit his tongue, he curbed his temper, he resisted temptation.

For two years, Daniel struggled with bedtimes, chores, homework, and back talk. Then, something miraculous happened. "One day, they came to my house and it was as if I had three different girls. My oldest was getting ready for her thirteenth birthday and we were planning a party. We put our ideas together, went shopping, and had a ball. No one screamed. No one complained about bedtimes. Occasionally there were words about homework, but other than that, life was calm. I was dying to ask the girls what gives, but I didn't.

"This went on for months and the months turned into years. I think that finally, over time, I realized what had happened. The girls stopped fighting me because they trusted me, they knew what the rules were, and I think they finally realized they were for their benefit. My eldest daughter understood this first, and the other two followed. I think in some way, the girls felt safe at my house. They knew that I would be home every night. They knew what they had to do. They also knew that I wasn't messing around when I told them something. I never yelled but when I said no, they knew that if they didn't listen, their phone was taken away, or they had to miss soccer practice for a week, or whatever. It worked. And somehow, they seemed to like having rules and standards and order and routine."

"Of course, they do," I said. "It makes them feel safe and protected. It makes them feel loved and wanted. Every girl wants her dad to protect her, no matter what she says. They can see through weakness, they know when they're manipulating a parent; they know your honesty and strength and rules mean you care about them."

The girls matured and when they scheduled trips to visit colleges, they wanted their father to take them. When they had boyfriend issues, they called him. He was the reliable, steady force in their lives because he had the courage to be a dad, to be the disciplinarian, and not to try to be his girls' older friend.

Play #6
Stay Committed

One of the great tests of a man's character is his ability to stay committed to a cause, a person, his work, or his beliefs. If you have been married longer than two or three years, you understand that marriage is something more than a prolonged honeymoon, it's a commitment.

Your kids need to learn this too—that many things in life involve *commitment*. When my eldest daughter got her first great job, she told me that, among my many failings as a mother, I had failed to warn her how *boring* work can be. Yes, well, that's life. There are days you won't want to go to work, or stay married, or be nice to your kids, but you need to do these things anyway. That's staying committed to your work, your spouse, and your family.

Dads can be great teachers of what it means to stay the course, hang in there, and gut it out, because that's part of what it means to be a man; heroes don't quit. They go the extra yard. They stay committed to their objective, their pledge, and doing what's right.

My mother lived next door to us for the last ten years of her life. After my father was moved into a nursing home, my husband

and son often helped her out. Very late one night, long after we were in bed, my husband took a phone call. It was my mother. He whispered to me, "Your mom's having some trouble so I'm going over. I'll call you if I need you."

At 7:30 in the morning I awoke and heard him coming through the door. He came to our bedroom and I noticed that he had his jeans on. "What happened?" I asked.

My mother, he said, had been having chest pains and was clearly in distress. He had called an ambulance and went with her to the hospital. He stayed with her through the night and decided to let me sleep. He knew that I didn't have to go into the office the next day; he did. But he let me sleep and took care of my mother.

After thirty years of marriage, I don't think I ever loved him more than I did that morning. That was commitment. It was commitment my son had seen as well, because he had heard his dad come home and overheard our conversation. And just before my son left for school that day I said to him, "Honey—that's what loving your wife well looks like. Don't ever forget."

If you want your son to have commitment like that, if you want your daughter to marry a man with commitment like that, show them how it's done.

These are your plays. Play. Pray. Be an honest man. Stay steady. Be firm and resolute. And above all, never, never, never give up on your kids or on being a great dad. Winning your kids is all about strategy. Make a simple strategy for each play and focus on those plays. I guarantee that if you do, you'll win at being your child's hero.

CHAPTER 7

Words: Power to Heal or to Hurt

Imagine watching your son on the ice at the state hockey tournament. With six seconds left and the game tied, the other team fires a shot and your son, the goalie, fails to block it because he slips and falls. The crowd groans and boos. Your heart sinks. You will be driving him home. What will you say to him?

You're driving your eleven-year-old daughter to her piano lesson, and she is in a foul, nasty mood. She just started her period, but you don't know that because her mother hasn't told you. Your daughter complains the entire trip about how her friends get to do more things than she does. You gently tell her that she's wrong and she jeers, "What the heck, Dad! You don't know anything. I mean, sometimes I just think you're stupid!" How will you respond?

Your son is a senior in high school and it's prom night. You loan him your second-hand BMW and at 2 a.m., you get a phone call. It's him and he's at the police station and your car has been totaled. You want to scream at him. Will you?

All of us have, at one time or another, said something to our kids or spouse that filled us with guilt and remorse. Why? Because we're human and we make mistakes, and sometimes we're so frustrated or upset or angry or sad or goaded that we just react without thinking.

But let me challenge you with something you need to remember: as a father, your words have an enormous, disproportionate impact on your family. You may not feel it, but your wife and children do, because you are the inevitable leader of your family. To your kids, you are *never* just an angry, sad, or frustrated guy, you're their dad. Every word you say has the power to wound or heal, crush or inspire.

In the Bible, we learn in the Book of Proverbs that, "A gentle answer turns away wrath but harsh words stir up anger. The tongue of the wise commends knowledge, but the fool gushes folly." And again: "He who guards his mouth and his tongue keeps himself from calamity."

Of course it's hard to give calm, controlled, gentle answers when someone is criticizing you or yelling at you, but think about it. Don't we all admire the man who keeps his head in a crisis? That's what a hero does, like the laconic cowboy whose few words, spoken low, can mean more than any amount of shouting. More than that, keeping your head means not saying those things you'll regret later. It improves the moment and leaves no bitterness in its wake.

Here's what you need to know. You have a choice from today forward to be the father that you want to be. So think about it.

What do you want to sound like? What do you want to teach your sons and daughters?

Think about your own father. Did he meet you with encouragement and patience or did he rake you over the coals with sarcasm and rage? Whatever your answer, think of how that made you feel. If you didn't know your father at all, put your rage against that phantom (which you probably feel) aside, and be the man your kids want you to be and that *you* want to be. Be the hero dad who is strong and understanding, who knows that wise words and a gentle heart can change a life.

The good news for dads is that your kids want you to help them, teach them, and encourage them, and every time you mess up and lose your temper or say the wrong things, they're ready to forgive you and move forward if you really want to. When it comes to you communicating better with them, they are on your side.

Consider your speech as a project. Your tongue is a powerful tool, but just like every muscle in your body, it needs training. So send it to training camp. You won't believe how much better you will feel and how much more influence you will have on everyone around you if you get full control of your words. In fact, you can even overcome anger, depression, and anxiety, and enjoy much greater happiness if you change the way you speak. If you doubt me, try this experiment for two weeks: every day pay a sincere compliment to your wife, your children, or your coworkers. You'll be amazed at the results—you'll have better relationships with those closest to you, and you'll feel better about life...and yourself! Granted, if you've been negative for a long time, you might need a month or two to change your outlook, but I promise, if you do this, it works. Simply changing the way you speak can change your life and your relationships with those around you; you can truly, as the hymn says, brighten the corner where you are.

Dads Are the Great Communicators

Women, as a rule, are more verbal than men. But in your family, *you* are the great communicator. Every day—wherever you are, even when you are absent—you communicate something powerful, because to your child nothing you say or do is neutral.

If you're not there, your son misses you, he might blame himself, and he might feel insecure (even if he takes pri1de in, for instance, you being a soldier posted overseas). Your absence is not neutral.

If you're at home but distant and uncommunicative, your daughter will suspect you don't care about her. Not engaging is not neutral either.

But if you come home from work, pull off your tie, and put on your baseball glove to play catch, your children will rejoice at their time with you (and you'll probably be happier too). Happiness is contagious. Happiness can come from a single word, a single smile, a single decision to spend quality time, or playtime, with those you love.

Here are a few examples of how this works.

Henry's father is in the military and deployed frequently, usually for periods of three to seven months. His parents make a point of letting their five-year-old son know that his father is leaving only temporarily and only because he has an extremely important job to do for his family and his country. That lessens the sting somewhat, and protects Henry from the misapprehension that he isn't loved. He still misses his dad, but he's reassured that dad is coming home, and that when he's home they'll make up for his absence with extra time together.

Ten-year-old Jenna's father is a stay-at-home dad who packs her lunch and puts her on the school bus. If dad is happy in the morning, she is happy. If dad gets angry because she knocked over the orange juice, she worries about it all day; her mood on the bus and at school is somber. That's what she's told me; it's what I've told her dad—and he was surprised. But that's a wake-up call for all dads. *Everything* you say and do—or don't say and don't do—matters.

José knows that his father loves watching him play soccer, and he is always aware of his presence: he feels relaxed if his dad looks relaxed, he feels nervous if his dad seems anxious on the sidelines. José's dad has no idea that how he stands—with his hands in his pockets or his arms folded defensively across his chest—has any influence on his son, until I bring it to his attention, but the effect on his son is enormous.

Leanne is an eighteen-year-old high school senior applying to colleges. Her father wants her to go to an Ivy League school, and though her grades are good (she is an outstanding student), her father's concern and worry that she might not have filled in her applications correctly or not done enough follow-up with the schools makes her tense and want to avoid any discussion of college at all; instead of being encouraged to do more, Leanne finds herself procrastinating, worrying, and wanting to defer any thoughts of college because it all seems too full of pressure. Dad has her best interests at heart, but he needs to back off a little, not pressure his daughter, and understand, and let her know that the college that accepts her will get an excellent student and an excellent person; the focus should be on her, not the school.

The bottom line for you fathers is quite simple: your words, body language, and presence can determine your child's outlook *every day*. Your kids might not tell you that but as their pediatrician that's what they've told me. They take everything you do and say as a reflection on them and how they should feel and react. Their identity is still forming and they are constantly looking to you to tell them who they are. As the great communicator dad, you need to make sure you tell them the right things.

The Four Essentials of Great Fatherly Communication

When talking to your children, you might want to think CAAR, which stands for correction, affirmation, attention, and respect—the four essential things that dads need to communicate. When you master these, talking with your children gets a lot easier.

Correction

When their kids are young, many fathers feel all they do is say "no." That's because two-year-olds spend most of their day toddling into perilous situations. Your job is to protect them, which means saying no over and over again.

The attention they require, and the tantrums they throw, can be challenging, no question about it. But this is the period in your child's life when you establish that when you say no, you mean no, and you have to do it without being harsh, because that can make a child withdrawn, sullen, and angry.

Here's a tip: when correcting a child, use the fewest words possible. Your toddler only knows a few words anyway, and as she grows older, she'll tune out long speeches of correction. All kids do this, because if you correct them at length they feel ashamed, hurt, and embarrassed, and in self-defense they try to stop listening. Using fewer words also keeps your temper in check. Anger has a habit of escalating, so cut yourself off. Stop talking. Leave the room (and don't slam the door).

Here are some situations you might face.

Your child runs onto the road—right after you told her not to.

Don't say this: "I can't believe that you are such a bad child! I just told you not to do that and you ran right out in the street just to spite me!"

Say this: "*Never* do that again!" in a firm voice and make eye contact. Put her in her room and let her cry a bit. When you return, tell her she must obey you and trust you. You are there to keep her safe.

Your eight-year-old son gets in a fight with his sister and hits her.

Don't say this: "You are such an idiot! Haven't I told you over and over not to hit? What's wrong with you? Why don't you just listen to me?"

Say this: "Son, you never hit girls—*ever*, especially your sister. I'm taking away your computer/television privileges for a week."

Your ten-year-old daughter is suspended from school for a day for bullying another girl.

Don't say this: "What a bad teacher! I can't believe that she would think that you would do something like this!"

Or this: "I can't believe that you would be so stupid as to bully someone. What's wrong with you? Don't you know that you can't be mean to people and get away with it?"

Say this: "I am terribly disappointed in you. You should never bully anyone; it's wrong. I'm taking away your phone for two weeks. You will come home immediately after school every day and we will work on a plan to help you never do this again."

If your child gets into trouble at school, see the teacher and find out what happened. Don't just instinctively defend your child, because if you let her off the hook without good reason, she'll feel empowered to behave badly later.

Also, avoid name-calling. You would never call someone at work stupid, so never do that within your family either. The point is *never* to demean your child; always to *correct* your child.

Your seventeen-year-old son gets a speeding ticket for driving ninety miles per hour on the highway.

Don't say this: "Son, you really screwed up this time! I worked so hard to help you buy that car and look what I get in return—complete disrespect and a ticket! You will pay that ticket, you know! I'm not going to! You have been disrespectful, dumb, and I'll bet you were just showing off! Why do you need to show off to your friends anyway? That's even dumber than speeding. You must be stupid to make such bad decisions and go out and almost kill yourself!"

Say this: "Son, I allowed you to drive the car because I trusted you to make mature decisions. You didn't. You will pay your fine and any extra rates we are charged for insurance on the car. Give me the car keys. You're grounded for a month, I'm sorry."

You find seven homework assignments in your son's backpack that he never turned in.

Don't say this: "Are you kidding me? I can't believe that you wouldn't follow through with your schoolwork! What's wrong with you? You were once such a smart kid. Keep this up and you'll never get into college!"

Say this: "Son, I need to talk with you. I noticed that you have seven homework assignments that you didn't turn in. Why?"

Good discipline will take a lot of self-control on your part. Always take a breath and remember that your goal is to briefly, effectively correct your children—not to frighten them, intimidate them, or demean them. If you yell at your child you actually take his attention off his misbehavior and onto your anger. If you know you have a bad temper, give yourself time before you respond.

Being a dad is a professional responsibility, and if you can control your temper at work, you can control it at home—period. If it's difficult, you just need to work harder—and here's how: depersonalize issues; approach them in a dispassionate, objective way (the way you might do at work); keep the focus on the future, on maintaining an open conversation with your child, because you don't want her to clam up for fear of sparking another parental outburst. The bottom line is, if you allow anger to take over your relationships with your kids, it will poison everything—including you, as you'll become angry with yourself and blame yourself for your children's mistakes, which are really only all part of being a kid. So take that deep breath for your sake and for theirs, and correct them with patience, calm, and love.

Affirmation

Dads are generally pretty good at affirming their daughters, but less good at affirming their sons, because they feel it's unnecessary. But both sons and daughters need your vocal affirmation—and guess what? You'll feel better after giving it too.

What do I mean by affirmation? I mean letting children know how intrinsically valuable they are to you (and to God)—that they are valuable to you because they are your children, not because of any prowess they might have—and how confident you are in their ability to handle challenges and situations, even if some, or many, require your help.

To express affirmation, use what I call "power words." They help build character. For instance, tell your son that he is (pick one): strong, kind, capable, patient, loving, lovable, valuable, considerate, smart, courageous, persistent, or tenacious. Be sure to invoke yourself and say, "I admire you, respect you, love you, believe in you, care about you, have confidence in you."

These are easy words of affirmation that you can slide into any conversation at any time. If you want to grow closer to your son or daughter *fast,* use them frequently, sincerely, and authentically without added sugar. (Sugar subtracts from their staying power.)

Here are some power words that you should avoid at all times. *You are*: stupid, worthless, lazy, an idiot, a b#*ch, an as#*&e, a baby, a weakling, a mama's boy, too chubby, fat, ugly, you'll never amount to much. Also never say, I can't put up with you any more, wish you were never born, hate you, dislike you, can't stand being around you, don't ever want to see you again.

Every conversation you have with your child leaves her feeling better or worse. Make it better.

I'd like to offer a word about teasing and sarcasm. Often fathers tease their children by calling them names or "poking" at them in fun. But think about this. Whenever you use sarcasm or teasing, there is always a grain of truth beneath the words. That's why people tease, because they take a small uncomfortable bit of truth and try to make it funny. But I have never met a kid who has enjoyed being teased by his father. I have, on the other hand, spoken to many who have been hurt by it. My advice: skip the sarcasm with your kids; there's too much at risk. And a kind word can do so much good. One of the wonderful things about children is that one sentence, one well-timed power word, or one wink of your eye at the right moment can change their lives.

Attention

From the first moment you hold your baby daughter, she will crave your attention, and as she grows older she will hang on your every word—even a simple "good morning"—and be constantly aware of your presence or absence.

Your son will be eager to have you see his first base hit, or hear his first trombone solo, or discuss his favorite movie, or play catch after work.

Your relationship with your children is dependent on the attention you give them—and they want your attention desperately because it makes them feel important and because they have important things they want to share with the most important person in their lives, whether that something is a movie or a personal triumph or simply the joy of playing in the yard or the basement.

Samuel was an only child. His parents never married and he alternated between living with his mother and his father during his elementary school years. Then his father moved away and he was forced to stay with his mother. He didn't want to, but because his father's new job involved lots of traveling, Samuel was told that he had to live with his mother. Samuel and his father had been close. They fished frequently in a local river. He loved evenings when they played catch in the tiny yard behind his father's trailer. Samuel told me, "We didn't talk much—but playing catch with my dad felt like I was warming up for a game at Yankee Stadium; it just felt special."

After his father left town, he felt lost. His father called him and did his best to stay connected, but much of his travel took him overseas and they lost phone contact for months at a time. Email and letters were all they had. "Over time, I guess I just got sadder and sadder. I don't know how else to describe it, except that I felt empty, like something really important was missing from my life.

I tried my best to not think about it, or about my dad, and I worked hard at school and tried to help my mom as much as I could."

When Sam was a junior in high school, something cracked. His grades fell, he started using pot and drinking a lot. He even got a girl pregnant. To his mother's dismay, he left home and dropped out of school. During those days, his mother told me she felt shocked. What happened to her nice boy? She was desperate, so she contacted Sam's father, who was working overseas, and pleaded with him to come and help. At first, Sam's father said that he couldn't return to the states—his work was demanding and his crew was short-staffed. But she kept calling and saying that she was worried for Sam's life. Sam's father finally returned. When Sam saw him, he was angry and defensive. Sam was afraid that he had let his father down. He felt ashamed. But his father never yelled at him. He simply came back to live near him and reintegrated himself into Sam's life. Over the next five months, Sam's life began to turn around. Sam didn't go to counseling—though his mother wanted him to do that—he just spent as much time as he could with his father. They even started playing catch again.

It took Sam's father a long time to understand the enormous effect that his presence—and absence—had on his son. He somehow thought that because he never married Sam's mother, and there was no divorce, that there would be no trauma when he left. He expected that Sam understood that he left for a job opportunity, not because of anything his son had done. But that's not how kids think. Mom and dad are mom and dad, whether they are married or not; and if they separate it is traumatic for the children. And kids need their father, no matter what. I've seen this played out over and over. The number of behavioral problems that could be cured or prevented by intact families, with mothers and fathers who pay attention to their children, is legion. Every daughter wants more attention from her father, and if she doesn't get it within a constructive, harmonious relationship, she'll get it in a destructive, disharmonious relationship with him—or with other men. Likewise, every son wants more attention from his father, and if he doesn't get it, he can behave like some variation of Sam.

Here are some key ways to give your kids the attention they crave.

Make eye contact. When you talk to someone and they don't bother to look at you, it's annoying. Maybe they're looking at their phone instead. It makes you feel unimportant. That's how your child feels, times ten, when you won't engage. So make eye contact, and recognize that a minute or two of full engagement now can—usually—satisfy a child, while ignoring him is stocking up frustration that will be expressed in the future.

Speak less, listen more. You have an advantage here. Moms like to talk. Dads are more often the strong, silent types. But that means you can be a good listener. Girls like to talk too, and if you are a good listener, your daughters will tell you a lot. Boys don't talk as much so those largely silent moments—like the ones Sam had with his dad, fishing or playing ball—can be more effective in building a healthy relationship than any number of forced conversations. (As an aside, boys have a particular aversion to being lectured repeatedly. With boys, actions most definitely speak louder than words. If you want to instruct them in something—even something like maturity—show them how it's done.)

Bottom line: be available, be engaged, be a good listener, and your children will grow in happiness and self-confidence under your care.

A minute becomes an hour. One of the most precious things about kids is this: time, for them, is magical; its quality and length can change depending on circumstances. When you give them a little bit of meaningful time and attention, that time expands in their minds. This means that if you spend five minutes a day in conversation with your daughter, she will grow up feeling that you were always there for her, ready to talk with her and share her day. A couple of hours a week fishing, playing catch, or working on a model airplane with your son will fill him with a sense of joy that he got to spend time with you. These are the memories your children will carry with them for life.

Respect

At some point, virtually every father will have a moment when he feels that his kids aren't treating him with proper respect. Even I have been astonished to hear kids call their good, smart, well-meaning fathers "stupid" or "losers." I've seen them roll their eyes in apparent exasperation or contradiction at something their father has said. It is frustrating, I know, but it happens all the time, and it can be disturbing to you and to other adults (like me).

Part of the problem—and it's a simple fact—is that our culture is cruder, crasser, and more vulgar than it has ever been, and it shows in our kids (and in a lot of adults).

Another part of the problem is that we believe we can't—or we simply don't want to—do anything about it. You come home from work and you're tired. The last thing you want to do is to get in conflict with your kids over their rude behavior; and maybe you see them so little that you just want to make your few hours together fun, even if it means putting up with behavior that you don't like. Other dads fail to correct their children because they think that all kids talk that way now, and, as I say, a lot of them do. But if you are a father who gives your kids a pass on rude behavior, stop. If they are going to respect anyone in the future—*including them-selves*—they need to start by respecting you.

Teaching respect doesn't have to be a battle, and it doesn't mean you have to act like a drill sergeant. In fact, you shouldn't, because quiet discipline, speaking in a strong, firm, respectful tone, is the best way to get the same response back. Kids respect strength, and self-control is a great example of strength—one that your kids will want to emulate if they see it in you.

So, if you want respect—and surely you do—show respect: to your wife and to your kids. Speaking and acting with respect shows kids what it looks like and how to do it.

Take the challenge of a month with no complaints, no negative comments, and a daily compliment to your loved ones, and see if you and they don't feel better for it. I think you'll find that respect begets respect. Even toddlers (two-, three-, and four-year-olds) can learn—and should learn—to say please and thank you and to make eye contact when they speak. Good manners can start early—and never get old.

Correction, affirmation, attention, and respect are the four key-notes of dads who are master communicators, and they reinforce each other. When you correct your child, speak to him not in anger but with respectful disappointment (your correction will be all the more deeply felt for its lack of anger). When you affirm your child's sense of worth, of value, look her in the eye so that she can see your sincerity. If you choose your words wisely, if you aim to be a respect-ful, attentive, affectionate, affirming dad who cares enough for his kids to be their calm and rational disciplinarian when necessary, you will be the hero that your kids want you to be in word and deed.

CHAPTER 8

Teach Them Courage and Truth

The hallmark of a hero is courage, and one of your tasks as a dad is to teach your children how to live a courageous life. That's something they expect to learn from you.

Being courageous has nothing to do with being physically strong or intellectually savvy (though courage can certainly make use of strength and smarts). *It is about having the internal fortitude to do what is right, true, and noble no matter the personal cost.*

Courageous men suppress their fears to avoid spreading anxiety to others. They never let fear keep them from doing the right thing. They never let excuses stand in the way of necessary action.

Courageous men are men who set standards, abide by them, and enforce them. They are models not just of bravery, but of self-discipline, self-restraint, tenacity, and wisdom gleaned from experience.

It is courageous men who are the answer to every social ill in our country—men willing to step forward and say: *enough*. Enough of irresponsibility; enough of fathers abandoning their children; enough of giving in to a popular culture that encourages bad behavior; enough of sons without role models and daughters without protectors. Irresponsibility has consequences—bad ones. Responsibility has consequences too—good ones. Good dads can make all the difference. Single mothers can be tough as nails, but they can never protect a daughter the way you can; boys can love their mothers, but they respect testosterone and they need courageous men to keep them in line and show them what courage really is.

The Power of No

One of the greatest powers you have as a father is the power of "no"—the veto of the head of the household—and the courage to use it. Let me give you an example.

For a while, Frank had coached his son Drew's soccer team. But Drew had real talent—so much talent that after two years Frank realized there was nothing more he could teach his son on the field.

Drew was so good that he was recruited to play on the varsity soccer team during his freshman year in high school. Drew knew that his father was proud of him, even though Frank's demeanor was generally stern and undemonstrative.

When Drew told his dad that August practices were mandatory for members of the varsity team, his father insisted that the family's summer vacation was even more mandatory; it took priority.

Drew was beside himself with anger, embarrassment, and worry that he would lose his varsity slot, that his coach would think he wasn't committed and serious, and that his friends would mock him. When he told his coach that he would miss a week of August training, his coach kicked him off the varsity squad. Drew told this to his father, who didn't flinch. "Well," said Frank, "that's his loss."

Drew refused to speak to his father for the next three weeks. He dreamed about running away from home, but didn't. He went with his family on their trip.

The following summer, the same scenario played out. The family went on summer vacation, Drew missed a week of training camp, and Drew, in his anger, refused to speak to his father, even though Drew's coach kept him on the varsity team, and allowed him to make up the lost training time.

Drew graduated from high school and played one year of Division One soccer, before deciding to focus on his academic interests. After graduating, he landed a great job with an engineering firm.

That winter, Frank called Drew with bad news. His mother had advanced breast cancer and the doctors told the family that she had less than a year to live. Drew felt the bottom drop out of his world. He adored his mother. She had stayed close to him throughout his high school and college years and always encouraged and supported him, especially during his fallouts with Frank. He didn't know how he was going to get by without his mother.

For the next six months, Drew drove home to be with his mother as often as he could. But just as her doctors had warned she might, she died within the year.

"As I look back on my high school years," Drew told me, "I am so very grateful that I spent as much time as I could with my mom. I will never get her back. And finally, I think I understand why my dad did what he did during those summers, insisting on family vacations. I was so incredibly angry at him then—and the parents of the other varsity soccer players were furious at him—but now, I feel so grateful that he put his foot down. He gave me extra time with my mother and siblings that I would never have had. And those weeks were very special. Yes, I was mad at my father, but deep inside, I cherished being with everyone." Drew paused. "Could it be that the parents of my teammates acted so nasty toward my dad because they were jealous?" That was a remarkable insight for a young man, and I could tell that Drew had learned some hard but very important lessons about life. He learned what was truly important and what really wasn't. He was grateful that his father had taught him.

"I know it sounds crazy, but I'm glad my father was tough on each of us when it came to spending time together. That's what I'm going to do for my family, for sure."

It took courage for Drew's father to insist on the family vacation and to accept his son's silent anger. But in saying "no" to misplaced priorities, he taught his son a tremendous, life-long lesson.

Courage and Truth
Doing what is right, true, and noble can be sticky business in a politically correct culture. I'm lucky because I don't operate

on political correctness; I do what medical science and clinical experience have taught me is best for kids. I have studied the needs of children for three decades and cared for thousands of them. I have been an eyewitness to what helps them and what harms them. And the things that help children always line up with what is right and true. And those things that harm children correspond to what is wrong and self-serving. Kids need dads who lead with moral courage.

I'm a great advocate of fathers, because I know how much you mean to your children. I know how courageous you can be, how self-sacrificing you can be, and also how often your role in the family is debunked or belittled in a culture that all too often has lost track of what is true.

When parents ask my advice on what movies or video games are acceptable, I usually say a variation of "father knows best," because you do. Fathers have a natural instinct to want to protect their family. You know the movies your children should and shouldn't see. You know how your fifteen-year-old daughter should dress when she goes to school or to the prom. You know how important it is to make family time a priority. So what prevents you from following your good fatherly instincts? It isn't lack of courage, I know that. It isn't lack of knowing what is right and what is wrong. Most likely it's because you've been indoctrinated to think that it's wrong to say no, that maybe father doesn't know best, and that you have to bend with our fallen culture. Never believe such nonsense. You are the dad. You are the hero. Be courageous. Stand for right over wrong. Stand up for your family at all costs.

I know that can be hard, especially in matters of sex and morality, because the standards that we used to take for granted have been turned upside down. And they've been turned upside down *not* because we've suddenly learned, scientifically or clinically, that promiscuity and sexual "experimentation" is healthy—in fact, *we know* just the opposite to be true. It's because there is an ongoing cultural war against traditional Judeo-Christian morality, and the anti-traditional morality forces are in the ascendant. I'll leave it to historians and others to tell us why that is so, but it is so, and I see the often tragic results almost every day in my practice. When I started practicing medicine, we had two or three sexually transmitted diseases to worry about. Now we have more than thirty; it's the least publicized epidemic in American medical history. It's not publicized because it is aided and abetted by many of the leading public institutions and "health" programs of this country, which push contraception as the panacea that it isn't and that encourage sexual activity and behavior that is, in fact, dangerous.

The culture might be going crazy, but you as a dad are not. You want your kids safe. You don't want your daughters sleeping around with men or women at college and you certainly don't want them assaulted. And when it comes to your sons, you want them to be strong, respectful, outstanding individuals because they are, after all, a reflection of you. You have a conscience; you have an interior sense of what is right and what is wrong, and I encourage you to use it. If you need a little help, here are a few guidelines that I've learned help kids.

What is right:

1. It is right for children to speak and act respectfully to parents and other adults.
2. It is right for children to learn about your religious views and your faith in order to learn to worship God.

3. It is right for children to show respect to their siblings and peers.
4. It is right for children to expect their parents to provide for their basic needs.
5. It is right for children to learn to work hard and value hard work.
6. It is right for children to learn to live in community with others (at school for instance or in church groups or on sports teams).
7. It is right for children to understand that they fit into a family and that the family does not revolve around them.
8. It is right for children to think of their body as the temple of their soul—not something to be harmed or defaced.
9. It is right for children to play outside, breathing fresh air, running, swimming, and having fun.
10. It is right for children to dream, optimistically, about their future.

Conversely, there are a few things that I have come to see as wrong (or harmful) for children to do.

What is wrong:

1. It is wrong for children to learn that being self-centered is good.
2. It is wrong for children to show frank disrespect to their parents or other adults.
3. It is wrong for children to willfully hurt others.
4. It is wrong for children to use foul language.
5. It is wrong for children to be sexually promiscuous.
6. It is wrong for children to be lazy.

7. It is wrong for children to cheat, lie, and steal.
8. It is wrong for children to look down on people because of their race or religion.
9. It is wrong for children to spend more time in front of an electronic device than in front of you.
10. It is wrong for kids to "experiment" with drugs.
11. It is wrong for kids to "experiment" with different sexual "identities."

I have learned that when kids do what is on the "right" list they grow up to have strong character and to be responsible, hard-working adults. And when they follow the list of "wrongs," I can almost guarantee that they are headed for some kind of trouble, whether physical, psychological, social, or economic. My list is not definitive. You and your wife can obviously make your own list. But set your standards and stand by them, because those standards are the guardrails of your children's future.

The decisions you make when your children are two, three, five, or ten are extremely important. But don't fall into the trap—as parents often do—of thinking that your teenagers don't need you so much, given that they seem so grown up, and might even be taller than you. Actually, your teenage son needs you now more than ever. He needs to see that manliness is courage and quiet fortitude and not following the gang or getting drunk or smoking or sleeping with girls. And if you have a beautiful sixteen-year-old daughter, you need to be vigilant about vetting potential boyfriends. Let her know that they need to respect her as a woman; they need to keep their hands to themselves—and yes, she may appear to snub your advice, and even slam her bedroom door when you say she can't date a certain boy. But good for you. Saying no takes a lot of courage and that's exactly what your daughter needs—and will respect. I promise, your daughter will grow up in time to thank you and adore you. She will ultimately respect you because she will value your strength, guidance, and wisdom that kept her from making a wrong decision, maybe a seriously wrong one.

When Courage Means Being Silent

The traditional hero is often a strong man of few words. There's wisdom in that.

Despite decades of propaganda that men should "share" their feelings, the fact is that there are many thoughts or feelings that should not be shared, that actually should be suppressed, and that certainly should not be acted upon. The courageous man trains himself to ignore these thoughts or feelings. He learns to control his temper, his attractions (sexual and otherwise), and his occasional moments of frustration, disappointment, or despair. He lives by his internal moral code—and that includes not only not burdening others with your problems, but not letting your feelings or thoughts get the better of you.

It also means making sure that what you say is guided by your moral beliefs. The good man puts moral truth before emotional temptation. That is true whether we're talking about words, thoughts, or deeds.

That can be hard advice to follow, I know, but it is part of being a man, a successful man, a heroic man, the sort of man we need more of, the sort of man you certainly want to be and can be because it is part of the interior of every man. Weak men routinely cave in to their own feelings and almost always end up miserable because of it. They end up regretting their weaknesses.

Strong men take pride in living by their moral code. If we think about what defines a man, that's a big part of it. And that can mean silently enduring, as Drew's father did, the anger of a son and the nasty comments of other parents. That sort of stoicism, self-control, and quiet confidence is part of being a hero dad. It is a source of strength—a strength that grows and inspires your children the more you use it.

Silence—the strong, self-controlled silence of a father—can speak volumes. Self-restraint and quiet courage might be rare virtues in our trash-talking, self-centered age, but they are virtues nonetheless.

Courage, Truth, and Your Kids

Fathers, though, are sometimes silent for the wrong reasons. They believe the lie that kids never listen to their parents.

If I have learned one thing about children of all ages in thirty years it is this: children *always* listen to their parents—and that can be a problem for many parents. When you tell your son that his grades are too low and he needs to improve them, he hears you. He may not improve his grades immediately (particularly if you butt heads with him often) but he will take your feelings to heart. If he isn't able to get better grades because of a learning issue, or some other reason he can't control, he will feel badly about himself. But if he can improve, he will, though it might take time. The best way to speed up the process is to balance your exhortation with encouragement. Say what you think and then move on; don't harp on the negative; find ways to encourage improvement.

If you have a daughter and she isn't gifted with tremendous physical beauty, be very, very careful. If she ever overhears you remarking about her figure, her homeliness, or comparing her to another girl, the damage to her sense of self-worth could take years to heal. What you say matters. Focus on your daughter's character strengths, and you will find that your relationship with her will deepen. (It will also remind her that character is what really matters.)

When a father speaks, what he says sticks for this reason: if you say something negative, it affirms, in the most powerful way, a child's own self-doubts; children assume you are a truth-teller. Conversely, if you say something positive, it can buttress a child's hopes and self-confidence; just make sure that your praise is grounded in truth, because children are quite expert at detecting lies.

Randy, a father with four children, worked for a large consulting firm. His job required weekly travel away from his family. Monday morning he would board a plane to a big city. He would stay four nights in a hotel and then fly home on Thursday. His schedule was grueling. And it was hard on his family. Randy did his best to engage with his children when he was at home, and he stayed connected with them by phone and Skype when he was on the road.

His son Tec didn't like his father being gone so much, but he accepted it. He knew that his father was working hard for the family. He respected his father's work ethic and that his dad made the extra effort to take him to hockey tournaments and on weekend ski trips.

Tec excelled in high school and was admitted to a very prestigious college. When Tec came home for Christmas break, I asked how his fall semester had been. "Good and bad, I guess. I really like the work and I've made some good friends but the other stuff is just a pain."

"What other stuff?"

"You know: the drinking, sex. It's honestly out of control." I wasn't surprised by Tec's openness. When my patients hit their teen years, I make a point of discussing sexuality and sexual activity; I also point out to them the facts—that every medical study affirms that the longer they delay sexual activity, the more likely they are to avoid sexually transmitted diseases (and, it should be noted, clinical depression).

"I wish I were surprised," I said, "but I'm not." As a pediatrician, I usually see my patients through their first year of college. I know what the general college atmosphere is like these days—and it's not good for kids.

"Here's what really bothered me," he said. "At our orientation, the school told us that every one of us students (at least the guys) got seven free condoms per week. If we wanted more, we needed to pay. I mean, I felt so demeaned; they just assumed we were animals with no self-control."

I was so proud of this young man. He was brilliant, ambitious, moral, and courageous. He believed that sex was part of marriage, not a party game.

He knew, as I tell all my patients, that condoms offer little protection against sexually transmitted diseases like HPV and Herpes. He and his fellow students were given no such warnings at his college. That's not unusual. Most colleges don't give students the facts about sex. They distribute propaganda.

Interestingly, I wasn't the only one who had tried to inoculate Tec against this culture. So had his father—and much more effectively. Randy had frank conversations with Tec about some of the things he had seen as a traveling businessman. "You know," Tec said, "he travelled all the time and he saw many of his work friends acting stupid—getting hooked on porn or drinking in hotel bars or having affairs and destroying their marriages. I respected him because he told me the flat out truth—and he lived by it too. And that's why I felt even more offended by what happened at school. They *wanted* me to go against everything that my dad had ever taught me. He stayed away from temptation—and so can I. My dad told me to wait until I got married, and he was loyal to Mom. Isn't that a better way? Why don't they teach that?"

That's a good question, but Tec was lucky to have a courageous father who set a good example and spoke the truth.

Tec's story had a happy ending. This strong young man—who soon became a professional athlete—wore a ring as a personal reminder to save himself for marriage. And sure enough, he got married. The night before his wedding he took that ring off and threw it as hard as he could into a lake; a new chapter of his life was about to begin and a new ring was going to take its place.

Teaching Your Kids Courage

As parents, we want our kids to be able to stand up for themselves, to say no to bad peer pressure, to say no to people who don't have their best interests at heart. When they are young, we tell them to avoid talking to strangers; when they are older we warn them of the dangers of drinking and drugs.

But at the same time, we often encourage our children and teens to be just like their friends, to fit in. We don't want our kids to suffer from poor "self-esteem," if they feel left out. Many parents go to enormous lengths to do this, not only buying their kids the "right" clothes, but following their friends on Facebook so they know which friends are the "right" ones to have. (Mothers, as a rule, are more attuned to social media and do this more often than fathers do.)

Fathers are in a great position to teach their children how to balance being accepted by peers without needing their approval in all things. And Dad, you should know, that as your kids get older, they're not looking to their peers for approval, they're looking to you—you are their model for what it is to be a grown-up. Despite the widespread myth that teens are more influenced by peer pressure than anything else, all the best research shows that this is absolutely not true. Affirmation, acceptance, and affection from a father is far more important to a child's self-esteem and self-worth than getting praise from peers. The most self-assured, self-confident teens are those who have the best relationships with their parents, especially when there is an active, engaged, strong father in the home.

If you want your child to have the strength to buck peer pressure, be strong, teach your values, show him—through your own actions, small and large—what courage looks like.

Here are a few ways to instill a spirit of courage in each of your children.

1) **Teach them where their real value comes from.** Children need to know—and parents, especially fathers, are the ones to teach them—that they have intrinsic self-worth. Never let your children doubt how much they mean to you. Never let them doubt, if you are a religious believer, that they were brought into this world by God, formed in his image, and born for a reason. Never let them doubt that their value is independent of any achievements, talents, or groups of friends they have; their value comes from being your son or daughter, from being, if you have a faith, a child of God. Never tire of telling your children this, especially as they become teenagers. Teens are almost always insecure and uncomfortable with their looks and their abilities. Just telling them that you love

them and that they are irreplaceable to you is enough. Keep it simple. Keep it truthful. And keep saying it. Children who avoid risky behaviors—and from a medical point of view, teen sex is at the top of the list—are usually children who have great relationships with their parents. And those parents almost inevitably include fathers who lead in courage and in truth.

2) Talk to them about being courageous. Once your children understand that their lives matter and have purpose, you can challenge them to be courageous in age-appropriate ways—ways that allow you to say, "I know this is hard but you can do it." Teach them to accept challenges rather than to avoid them. Teach them to tell the truth and to stand by it. Teach them to take responsibility for their actions—including the bad ones, and to accept just punishment when appropriate rather than trying to weasel their way out of it (letting children get away with things always sets a very bad precedent). Teach them to stand tall, politely and firmly, for their beliefs.

When your children show courage—when your high school son talks to his chemistry teacher about the test he failed or your high school daughter tells a boy to back off when he pressures her to have sex—congratulate them on doing the right thing, and let them know how proud you are of them.

3) Tell your own story. Nothing will give your children more courage than stories from your own life about how you triumphed over adversity, how you worked hard and saved money for school, or how your tenacity finally paid off in a rewarding career. They will also want to hear about how you lived by your values and avoided temptation. When speaking to your sons, the most vital thing is to teach them the quiet heroism of self-control. If you're a married dad, this might be slightly easier, because your son will have a wonderful role model of what fidelity in marriage means. If you're a single dad, it can be a little harder, but not at all impossible. The key thing is to underline that virtue is its own reward, that pornography—while it might be ubiquitous—is a vice (and a dangerous one), and that a man proves his mettle by his powers of self-control and by his living of a virtuous life; it is a hard task, which is why it is the true test of a man. Even if your own early life was marked by promiscuity, don't talk about that (because it will only make it seem as though it's excusable) and don't feel like a hypocrite for talking about virtue now. The fact is, sexual promiscuity today is even *more* dangerous because of the proliferation of sexually transmitted diseases. Tell them you understand temptation, but also teach them about the importance of not giving in to it. If your past is checkered, you can keep this vague, because as far as your teenage children are concerned, there are two people on the planet that they believe are not sexually active and you are one of them. Believe me, they don't want to hear about it.

Your daughters require a different and less direct approach. They don't want to hear about how you might have been tempted, because they don't want to see you in any way as a sexual being. As the opposite sex, it makes them feel odd, especially if you are a single dad. So talk to your daughters about what you want for them and how they can (and must) have courage in dealing with young men, but don't talk about yourself. Remember, you are their hero and protector, their guardian and source of wisdom. They should never see you as a hormone-driven teenager.

4) **Live it.** Kids want to emulate their heroes, and you're hero number one. Your daughter needs to see you control your temper when your wife is angry with you. Your son needs to see you refuse to tell lies. What they don't need to see is you joking with friends

about cheating on your taxes or at work. For them that won't be a joke, it will simply sabotage your attempt to set a good example.

Sometimes the best example can seem the hardest: standing by your principles when your kids would rather you bent the rules. I have heard many parents lament that they give in to their teen's wishes because they simply didn't want to argue. Don't do this. It almost always turns out badly for the kids.

Several years ago I was speaking with a single father, Greg, who had three daughters and the oldest was fourteen years old. His fourteen-year-old went to a private school, got good grades, played three sports, and was, overall, a star. But Greg had one problem: her friends' parents.

On the weekends, the girls would have regular parties at one of their homes, and to Greg's dismay, the parents allowed the kids, who were all underage, to drink as long as they surrendered their car keys.

Greg didn't want his daughter to attend the parties but she pleaded with him, telling him that she would be seen as an outcast and a loser if she didn't go. Of course, he didn't want that to happen. He spoke with the other parents who told him they were just being realistic: the kids were going to drink anyway and at least here they would be supervised and not allowed to drive.

Greg told me he felt he "had no choice" but to let his daughter attend the parties. He hated her drinking but felt bullied into letting her go. At one of these parties a boy tried to seduce Greg's daughter. She pushed him away. Later in the evening, the boy got mad, cornered her alone and almost raped her. She was terrified and didn't want to tell her father what happened.

Greg learned of the assault several months after it happened and was beside himself. He wanted to press charges against the boy but this would have meant telling on the parents who hosted the party. He found himself in an enormous mess. The worst part of it was the mental and emotional harm that had been inflicted on his daughter.

Fathers, if you read this book and remember only one thing, let it be this: stand up for your kids. Have the courage to do the right thing no matter what the cost. You will save them from themselves and from others who intend only bad things for them. If Greg had had the courage to say no to his beautiful daughter, she would not carry the scars that she will now always have, scars that will make it hard for her to trust men, including her father who, inevitably, she will think didn't love her enough to protect her. That's what girls do when they get into trouble. They look to their fathers. And she will wonder why dad, her protector, failed her. Girls do this because they see you as their hero. Never forget this.

Any father can live a courageous life, and your kids are worth every sacrifice you make on their behalf. Courage is a virtue, and not coincidentally, the Latin word *virtus* means "manliness, the spirit, or strength of spirit required to be a man." If you allow it, courage can define you as a man and better still, get passed on to your children. Make sure that your sons and daughters have a chance of becoming courageous men and women. Be that courageous, heroic man. They might not show it initially, but they will respect you for your courage, and when they become adults they might even say thank you for it.

CHAPTER 9

God Is Called Father And So Are You

You might wish you were the world's wealthiest man or the wisest, or a movie star, or a life-saving doctor, or the world's greatest pitcher or quarterback or basketball player, or maybe even a secret agent or president of the United States. But whatever your wish, it would be less than what God is, and yet what name does God prefer above all others? *Father.* Let that sink in for a while. The Creator of all, the source of all power and wisdom, has one great desire: to be called *Father.* You share that name with God. He expects you to be worthy of it.

The Name of the Father

So what are the qualities that God himself associates with fatherhood? Let's start with the Hebrew word *Abba,* which means "daddy" and connotes warmth, tenderness, and approachability. We don't often think of God this way, but it is one of the names he gives himself. God tells us that we are to call him Abba, which is an assurance that we can rest safe and secure, comforted and protected, accepted and cherished, in his arms.

The million-dollar question for you, my friend, is this: are you approachable, tender, and warm with your children, as God means you to be? Does your kindness give them a sense of security? If your father was kind and often at home you are probably comfortable with these terms. If he wasn't, you might feel uncomfortable and defensive. But don't be. If you had a bad relationship with your own father, put him aside, and remember that God is the Father of all, and with his help you can be the good man, the good father, you want to be. God abandons no man who wants his help, and his patience with us is a mirror of the patience we as parents must sometimes have with our own children.

Bradley was the product of a broken home. He remembered how his mother cried herself to sleep many nights after his father left. Needless to say, this was a painful memory for a young boy. When Bradley was ten, his mother remarried. Bradley's stepfather was a very nice man, but Bradley had trouble accepting him as any sort of father. He considered him an outsider, not really part of the family, and felt a desire to drive him away.

At fifteen, Bradley became a hellion. He took drugs, ran with the wrong crowd, slept with as many girls as he could, and essentially tried to tell his parents to go to a dark place where the sun wouldn't shine. He was mad. He was sad. And he wasn't going to let anyone hurt him, or so he said.

When his grades plummeted, Bradley's mother talked to his teachers and counselors. She did everything she could to help him. Likewise, his stepfather tried his best to bond with Bradley, taking to him to baseball games and offering to take him on a fishing trip, but Bradley would have none of it. Drugs obscured his thinking, and finally, his parents gave him an ultimatum: either you live clean or you leave the house. His answer came immediately. He left.

He floated from friend's house to friend's house. Occasionally he would come home and stay clean for a while, but then he would leave again. At seventeen, Bradley had a car and this time he figured his break from his family would be forever. "When I left at seventeen, I wasn't as afraid," Bradley told me. "I had been homeless before and knew that I could survive. Maybe I was kidding myself, but I believed that someone somewhere owed me something and as soon as I got whatever that was, I would be okay.

"I would go to school during the day and then after school, I'd shoot hoops at an abandoned court with some friends. At night, I drove to a Walmart parking lot and stayed in a back lot. I'd eat food I snuck in my backpack from school and this would be dinner. Then I'd sleep in my sleeping bag in the back of my car. Was I scared? Yes. I was a kid. And it got scarier because every night I noticed a car would pass by mine and slow down. It never stopped, but I got pretty scared. I was sure that whoever was in that car was going to do something bad to me. When I met a friend playing basketball and he was all black and blue because an older boy had beaten him up during a drug deal, something in me snapped. I was nearly eighteen then, but I was scared. I knew that could be me and I decided to go home."

Bradley drove home and found his mother upstairs. She burst into tears at the sight of him. He asked permission to stay at home and she said yes. As he was sitting in his bedroom, Bradley heard his mother call his stepfather. Within an hour, his stepfather was home talking to him.

When he saw his dad, Bradley cried like a baby. He was overwhelmed with shame, remorse, embarrassment, and unresolved anger. Bradley knew he had behaved like a jerk to a fundamentally good man. And for what? Bradley had no real clue—only that drugs had led him to theft, which had led to harder drugs, which had led him to sleeping in a Walmart parking lot where he might have been beaten or worse, and all because he was angry about something that he couldn't, at that moment, explain.

Bradley's stepfather listened quietly to his son's story. "Dad," Bradley said, "I was really scared. Many nights I couldn't sleep and I would see car lights flashing on the roof of my Subaru. I thought that these guys were going to kill me. And then, when I saw my buddy's face with the bruises, that was what got me. I knew that I had to come home."

When Bradley had told him everything, his stepfather said, "Your mother and I love you, Bradley. I know you don't believe me, but it's true. Your dad left you a long time ago and I'm not him. But I have always loved you as my son. That's what allowed me to be so hard on you. I couldn't sit and watch you kill yourself with drugs. No good father could do that. And you need to know something else, Bradley. Those car lights every night? Those were mine."

The good father is warm, approachable, and protective. Bradley's stepfather watched over him every night to make sure that his homeless son was safe in the Walmart parking lot. Bradley's father—a good man protecting an out of control, angry boy—let his son go, but he was always watching over him, ready to welcome him back, as God is with each of his children.

Responsibility Demanding Respect

When we think of fatherhood, we rightly think of responsibility. Joseph, the husband of Holy Mother Mary in the Bible, was even give care of the infant Jesus, *of God made man.* Joseph—a humble and simple man—was picked to raise the Jesus who was God and a sinless man all in one. Talk about responsibility!

You don't have *that* weight of responsibility, but you do have responsibility enough. And here's something that you might not know: your children love it when you demonstrate responsibility. Why? Because that's what heroes do. They're the ones who always stand up to be counted; they're the ones who always do their duty; they're the ones who never let people down.

Taking responsibility is something that often separates you from your children, because you handle things they're not ready to handle—and they like that. Many parents don't understand that their children want them to be responsible adults. They don't want their parents to act like cool kids, because they know that kids are ignorant. They want a grownup in the room, someone with wisdom and experience who can protect them so that *they* can relax and be kids. Their security depends upon your responsibility.

Being responsible may not be a big deal to you, but it is for them. When you follow through and do what you say you are going to do, they learn that they can trust you. And when they can trust you, they can look up to you. And when they look up to you, they respect you. And respect from your children is critical to a healthy relationship with them.

Sons imitate what they respect. If a son sees his father as weak, unreliable, and forgetful, he will distance himself from his dad because he won't trust him. But the son who can trust his father

moves closer to him. He knows that his father is dependable. That
leads to respect, and from respect comes imitation.

My husband is stubborn, strong-willed, and occasionally impa-
tient. He is also deeply religious. His father was the same. But when
we first married I saw some stark differences too.

My father-in-law worked endless hours as a small town physician. He always had two things in his car: his medical bag and a
trunk filled with Bibles. He made house calls; he served widows,
children, and prisoners; and he consoled the dying. He was born
to love through practicing medicine.

As a boy, my husband admired that his dad was a hard worker,
but it also meant that he didn't see him as much as he might have
liked and they didn't do much together, because my husband is
extremely outdoorsy and his father wasn't.

When my father-in-law's pulmonary fibrosis suddenly worsened and he was on his deathbed, my husband stayed with him,
sleeping in a cot by his side. His dad was only seventy, and he had
been my husband's chief source of medical advice in his own practice. Now he was gone.

After his dad's death, my husband slowly changed into someone more like his father. He spent less time in the woods and more
time at his work. He made house calls. He helped men who were
in prison. He served at the local soup kitchen and several years ago
a large box arrived at our front door. When I opened it, I saw an
enormous stack of blue paperback Bibles with his father's name
stamped on the inside cover: if anyone ever needs a Bible (in his
father's favorite translation), he'll have one to offer.

I have seen this happen in other men too. After their fathers die,
many sons become more like their dads. Why? I think it is because

the respect and admiration a son feels for his father intensifies after his father's death—after the son is forced to reconcile himself to mortality and to recognize the full strength of his father's example. The father lives on in his son.

And that's important in more ways than one, because for your children to grow up to be healthy adults, they need to respect you. Respect is not commanded, it is earned. You need to show them, through your actions, through your responsibility, that you are a hero.

Some fathers are fabulous dads but they allow their children to talk to them as though they were classmates. I hear young kids yell at their fathers, call them names, or give them snide looks. Don't allow your children to treat you this way. This is wrong—to you and to your children. I have seen brilliant men apologize for making their children angry; they excuse their children for yelling at them. I have watched good men stand by and allow their teenagers to call them "stupid" or a "jerk."

Commanding a healthy fear from a child is foreign to most modern fathers, but a *healthy* fear is a good thing, because it is nothing more than a sign of awe and respect, of not wanting to do wrong before a judge who really matters. (Remember how God says in Proverbs "the beginning of all wisdom is fear of the Lord.") Without that healthy sense of fear, a child can become disrespectful, and a child who is disrespectful certainly doesn't feel adoration for his father, and chances are he won't trust him either, because he will assume he is weak. Never let your children demean you with their speech or behavior. Tolerating that is not being understanding, compassionate, or "connecting" with them. In fact, the weaker you are with them, the less you meet their innate expectations of what a father should be.

Every good father should elicit a sense of awe from his children, because that's what heroes do, and that's what you need to do so that your children grow up polite and respectful, so that they learn what is acceptable and unacceptable behavior. You are their moral teacher, and a moral teacher does not connive at or passively indulge in behavior that is rude, insulting, vulgar, and wrong, and that can only help shape rude, self-centered, irresponsible adults. Teach your children well—for they are the Americans of tomorrow, for good or for ill. As parents, the next generation is in our care. We have a responsibility to guide them on the right path.

Restrained Power

Power and responsibility are always linked.

Men have power: physical power, of course, but also the cognitive power that comes from being solution-oriented.

In a man, the responsibility that comes with power is a matter of self-control. A man needs to control his temper, his sex drive, his thoughts, and his actions. Our culture, when it was healthier, made this easier, because it expected men to watch their language, to dress and behave with decorum, to abide by the standards of Judeo-Christian morality, to perform what was regarded as their duty as men. This is no longer the case, but it remains true that God has given every man the power of self-control. It is there, like a conscience; it just needs to be exercised.

The best definition of restrained power—and its importance—probably came from a military man, General Robert E. Lee. Lee was known as a brave and daring officer, but also as a wise and kindly man. He wrote:

The forbearing use of power does not only form a touch-stone, but the manner in which an individual enjoys certain advantages over others is a test of a true gentleman.

The power which the strong have over the weak, the employer over the employed, the educated over the unlettered, the experienced over the confiding, even the clever over the silly—the forbearing or inoffensive use of all this power or authority, or a total abstinence from it when the case admits it, will show the gentleman in a plain light.

The gentleman does not needlessly and unnecessarily remind an offender of a wrong he may have committed against him. He cannot only forgive, he can forget; and he strives for that nobleness of self and mildness of character which impart sufficient strength to let the past be but the past. A true man of honor feels humbled himself when he cannot help humbling others.

If you want to know how to be a good father, to lead by example, to show your sons (and daughters) what real manliness is (the restrained use of power), to discipline with a brief word rather than with shouting—it's all there.

But we can look higher, too. We can see in God a restrained use of power. God wants us to love him, but in the end he does not command us or force us. Yes, he puts our faith to the test, but in the end, his love for us is sacrificial. He allowed himself to be crucified for our sins. He does not, thank goodness, expect you to make that sacrifice, but he does expect you to sacrifice yourself for those you love.

One of the great rewards for fathers is that the more your children see you as a man of courage, humility, patience, self-control, and warmth, the more they will want to adopt these qualities as their own.

Your children start their lives with you as their hero. You can maintain that good reputation easier than you might think. It starts with being responsible, with being as good as your word. If you promise your son you're going to play catch with him Thursday after work, do it.

It's also important to be warm, loving, and approachable—even if you don't feel that way. You can make it easier for your children to talk with you simply by lowering your voice (which will make you seem less intimidating), making eye contact, and actually listening to what they say. Skip the teasing and the sarcasm, which creates distance rather than engagement, and treat their thoughts and feelings with respect. They want to trust you, so be worthy of their trust, and set age-appropriate rules—including curfews and dress codes—that underline how much you care about them and that you want them to be safe. Finally, exhibit the self-control of a hero. You might not think your children will notice, but they do. They see your weaknesses, your temptations, your stumbles, but they also notice when you steer clear from temptation, when you refrain from getting angry, when you avoid that drink that makes you tipsy or unpredictable (which frightens or embarrasses them), when you refuse to watch a movie or show that might be morally objectionable. The things you don't do or say—your self-restraint— can be even more powerful than the things you do.

Most of all keep faith with your children, believe in them. A father's faith can motivate a child for life. That was the experience of former Green Bay quarterback Brett Favre.

Delivering his acceptance speech at his induction into the NFL Hall of Fame, Favre spoke with deep emotion about his deceased father who had coached him in high school and who was, Favre said, a man who was "short on praise and long on offering advice on improvement." His father often stayed after football practice to lock up the school and turn off lights before the two headed home in his truck.

After Favre's last high school game, he overheard his father telling three other coaches, "I can assure you one thing about my son. He will play better, he will redeem himself. I know my son. He has it in him."

That expression of faith meant everything to Favre. It changed him. From that moment, he did everything he could to make his father proud as a football player. Favre, in his speech, looked heavenward and said, "I want you to know. Dad; I spent the rest of my career trying to redeem myself." After a pause, Favre said, "I spent the rest of my career trying to redeem myself and make him proud. And I hope that I succeeded." Then the great football player gave in to the tears that were choking him.

Nothing can replace a father's love. "Father" is a word of such profound significance, meaning, and hope that it was the first word Jesus uttered when he was crucified. It was the cry of a man who agonized for the people he loved. Those people are us. And the Father he cried out for watches over us still, just as you, in your children's imaginations, will always watch over them, just as Brett Favre's father was always watching over him. Be worthy of your children. Be like your own Father, the one who is in heaven.

CHAPTER 10

The Hero's Winning Triumvirate: Perseverance, Forgiveness, Engagement

In chapter three we met Dick Hoyt, who has raced with his disabled son Rick in an amazing 247 triathlons (six of which were Ironmen), seventy-two marathons (including the Boston and Marine Corps Marathons), and a combined bike-run across the United States covering 3,735 miles in forty-five consecutive days.

But that's only part of the story. Rick's parents were told—by doctors and school administrators—that their son would never be able to learn, to communicate, or to have any idea of what was going on around him. Rick and his parents proved them wrong. Today, Rick is a graduate from Boston University, and though wheelchair-bound, he lived there, as a student, independently.

Dick Hoyt never let doctors or teachers dissuade him from what he knew to be true about his son. As he told me, "I could look at Rick's eyes and I knew that he understood everything people were saying around him."

Although schools wouldn't take Rick, his parents taught him his letters and numbers, read to him constantly, and had Tufts University design a computer that allowed Rick to tap out words. "I'll never forget his first words to us," Dick said. "We were watching a Boston Bruins game and Rick wrote 'Go Bruins' on the screen. We almost cried."

I asked Dick, "Were you or Rick ever so exhausted in a race that you thought of quitting?"

His answer was immediate. "Never. Not once." The rewards, he told me, were too high: "No man can be closer to another person than I am with Rick."

Dick Hoyt's life as a father can be summarized in two words: love and tenacity. Love for his son brought out Dick's tenacity, which changed both their lives for the better. It wasn't just running marathons, it was refusing to give up on his son when doctors and schools told him his case was hopeless, when race authorities (at first) refused to let him participate. Dick never took no for an answer. He fought for his son, and fights for him in every race he runs. Perseverance, which is a characteristic I've noted in all strong fathers, is one of the best traits a man can have; it is what makes you win; what allows you to finish the race; and why your family can rely on you through thick and thin.

Every father can be as close to his son as Dick is to Rick, because every dad is capable of that same love and tenacity. Dick told me so himself. "It's easy," he said. "Just take your kid to a movie or throw a ball with him." He's absolutely right. Getting closer to your kids is easy. All you have to do is stay engaged and stick with it.

All Heroes Persevere No Matter the Challenge

Think for a moment of the man (or woman) you would describe as your hero. It is probably someone who never gave up; who did the tough work that others shirked; who had the determination to press ahead no matter the obstacles.

Every man has these qualities—summed up, for me, in the word perseverance—but few men actually realize their full potential. I've seen, and you probably have as well, that too many men simply meander through life waiting for others to take a lead, or they think the effort to succeed isn't necessary or even possible.

It's a problem that's getting worse, because, unfortunately, it's often encouraged by women. Thanks to the sexual revolution, which separated sex from marriage and abolished (up to a point) traditional sex roles (including the man being head of the household), many men feel no need to commit—to a wife or to children—or to lead their families. Instead, they wait for a girlfriend to say when it's time to get married. Or they let their spouse decide when it's time (or not) to have children. Or they let their wife lead the family; and while there's absolutely nothing wrong with cooperating with a spouse on making important decisions, some men have simply checked out: they assume that mom is the center of the family and dad's role is pretty much limited to earning a living and staying out of the way.

But that's not the right path for you or for any man. It's not the path of a hero. It's not the sort of husband most wives want or that all children need. They want a hero who can size up a situation, see what needs to be done, and act for what is right and good.

Every child desires to have a father as devoted as Dick Hoyt. Every child wants a dad who perseveres—who is willing to play or to listen, when he'd really much rather just sit on the sofa and watch TV or go to bed. All children want a dad who can take on the burdens of the adult world so that they don't have to. They want your protection, they want your leadership, they want your total, unbreakable love and commitment.

Your children notice if you give in to fatigue, if you surrender to a gloomy mood, if you slack off at work (they can tell) or at home (they can see). They want a dad with the self-discipline and dedication to carry on no matter what. They want you to be a hero. Ultimately, that's what you want to be as well—the hero who puts others first, because doing the right thing is its own reward.

John Denney is a long snapper for the Miami Dolphins. As a twelve-year veteran NFL player, he knows the importance of being level-headed and steady in a crazy world. John is a successful husband, father, and pro football player, but also humble, gentle, and wonderful to talk with; a man whose priority isn't himself or his ego or his career, but his family. As he was quick to stress to me, his parents get the credit for his virtues, because they brought him up with the idea of always being respectful, loving life, and putting the needs of others before your own.

His parents were hardworking and religious parents (he remembers spending not just Sundays but Wednesday nights in church), and were devoted to their children. Unlike many of the players I've talked to, his family was close-knit; he had a happy home life; he wasn't a rebellious teenager; and he enjoyed spending time with his parents and his parents' friends.

My sense was that he was immune to the temptations that lead so many football players astray. I asked him how that happened.

"Honestly," John told me, "I never realized that people spoke crudely until I graduated from college and came to the NFL locker rooms."

"You mean in high school and college you didn't see kids behaving badly?"

"I know it's hard to believe, but I didn't. My parents were incredibly respectful to us kids and to one another; and their friends were the same way. When I went off to college at Brigham Young, the same thing. Everyone expected us to act respectfully and we did."

"Do you feel now that your parents raised you in a bubble?"

"Yes, but it was a great one. I knew what was expected of me and I knew what my parents expected of themselves. They never expected us, as kids, to do or be anything that *they* weren't. My father set the standard for all of us—and we followed. He was an incredibly hard worker. And he was consistent in what he did."

There was a word that grabbed me. His father was *consistent*—holding high standards for his kids and himself, year in and year out. That's how a great father shapes and leads a great son.

His father trained him to always take the hard road—that is, to work hard, to act with discipline and self-control, and to remain faithful to what is right and true.

Raising a man of excellent character like John Denney requires the work of a hero. It is hard. It means living against the grain of the surrounding culture. But John's father was wise in surrounding himself and his family with like-minded friends and the support of his church; he put God first, family second, and work (though he was very hardworking) third.

John's father had the ultimate virtue: courage. He had courage to live by his principles, and by his faith, rather than by the shifting (and nowadays usually terribly harmful) tides of popular culture. He was a leader, not a follower.

I asked John what he wished for his own kids. He said, "I hope they'll grow up to be aware of other people. I don't want them to be self-focused, but considerate of the needs of others. Also, I want my kids to be independent and self-reliant. I want them to work hard, just like my father showed me. He worked hard and made his way and I want my kids to learn the same thing so that they don't have to depend on others to do what they can do for themselves."

As an NFL professional, John could make life very easy for his children. But he doesn't spoil them, because he cherishes the gifts that his father gave him: a sound work ethic and concern for the welfare of others. His father should be mighty proud.

Perseverance and Forgiveness: Why They Go Hand in Hand

Let's be honest: no one admires a quitter—and that "no one" includes your wife and children. When roadblocks appear in your family life, they expect you to clear them. That means taking the initiative—even when the initiative is a simple reconciliation after an argument. Your kids (including teens) don't have the cognitive ability to argue with you as an equal, but they are desperate to be restored in your sight after a quarrel. Similarly, while you might prefer your wife to initiate reconciliation, she and your children will always look to you first—not necessarily as a confession that you were wrong, but because they instinctively look to you as a leader, as the hero whose words and actions can heal.

Saying "I'm sorry" can be hard—especially if your father never said it to you. But there are few words in your vocabulary (beyond

"I love you") that will have more power in your child's life. Those words are powerful because they are a statement of responsibility and a testimony of love. And a hero is not afraid to use them.

It is inevitable that *every father hurts his child* in some way. Maybe you yell when you shouldn't. Maybe you made a sarcastic comment you now regret. Maybe you forgot to go to a soccer game. Maybe you were late to your son's birthday party or missed it altogether. Maybe you suffered through a divorce and moved out of state. Or maybe you abandoned your daughter, because you thought her mother was better off without you. No matter what you did or how deep the pain resonated with your son or daughter, do not be afraid to deal with your mistakes. The first and most important part of reconciliation is to admit what you did and how much it hurt. It is the only way to free yourself from a lifetime of guilt and estrangement from your child.

Guilt can weigh good men down. When a father refuses to admit his mistakes or own them, he lives alone in a dark world of shame and hurt. If you abandoned your child, deal with it now, for her sake as well as yours. You need to confront your worst mistakes. You can begin by forgiving yourself, because you can't undo the past. But what you can do is make amends, as best you can, with those you have hurt.

If you have a faith, ask God for forgiveness. I promise, it works. It will lower your anxiety, give you peace, and improve your relationship with your children. I've seen it happen many times.

When you make amends with a child or a teen, do it face to face, make eye contact, and do it without distraction. Even so, very often, children won't respond immediately. If your child pretends not to hear you or even gets mad at you, that's normal. Forgiving a father (or mother) takes time, so give your child time.

The important thing—the *very* important thing—is that your child knows that you care about him; that your parental love is constant, no matter the mistakes you have made in the past and or the mistakes you will almost certainly make in the future because you're human.

Let me give you a peek inside your child's mind for a moment. Children who hurt inside act mean. First graders who have their feelings hurt either cry, say bad things, or strike out at a parent (or someone else). Teens who feel lonely, sad, or anxious often act nasty at home. If your thirteen-year-old daughter slams doors and refuses to hug you, it isn't because she hates *you*; it's much more likely that she hates herself, and needs you to persevere in loving her. Children and teens have a hard time expressing their feelings, which is why those feelings can come out awkwardly—as in a refusal to do homework or in sulking. Let me say it again: *never take your child's behaviors personally.* Whether that child is two, twelve, or twenty-five, most often the trouble is that your child is hurt or confused or simply immature and doesn't know how to express himself. It's probably not your fault. But you can help him.

The most heroic act you can perform is to face your son (or daughter) in a calm manner and apologize for any harm you've done them. If you can, be specific; if his internal misery is a mystery to you, you can keep your apology broad and all-encompassing. Even though the chances are excellent that you are *not* responsible for your child's hurt feelings (or at least not all of them), your apology will provide more reassurance and healing than you can likely imagine.

I know, asking a child for forgiveness is no easy task. Many fathers don't see the need, or don't think they, as fathers, have done anything wrong, or feel that if they hurt their children's feelings, it's because the children deserved it for misbehaving; and fathers certainly don't want to give their children the upper hand in any ongoing family dispute.

It takes heroic effort to man up and make that apology, doing it for all the right reasons, because reconciliation within a family is more important than winning an argument or standing on one's innocence or guarding one's pride. If you make reconciliation a priority—if you have the courage to apologize—you'll feel stronger, not weaker, because you have conquered your ego. And your children will admire you all the more, because they will know you care, and because *they* know how hard it is to apologize.

My father was a man of courage who had to endure a lot. In his mid-sixties, he developed early onset dementia. It was crushing to watch, but it also revealed my father's strong character in different ways. Dementia stripped him of his anger and bad temper, but in the early days of his disease, as he realized what was happening, he cried often, sometimes for days. Then confusion set in. He wandered around the house almost like a child, sometimes asking where his bedroom was.

Eventually, he started to laugh again at simple jokes, which made the disease somewhat more bearable for all of us. He wasn't himself, but I could see glimmers of happiness in his eyes. We could walk and talk together, and laugh.

One day, we had a walk that I will never forget. He was shuffling along, holding the wall rail that ran down the hall at his nursing home, and I had my arm looped through his. We were talking about something silly and irrelevant when all of a sudden he stopped in his tracks. I was startled, "Dad, what's wrong?"

He looked at me with a stare that said, "I'm really here now." I was astonished. Then he spoke some extraordinary words.

"Meg," he began, "am I forgiven?" His words stunned me. I saw tears rolling down his face. I didn't think he needed to be forgiven for anything but said, "Well, yes, Dad. Yes, you are forgiven." He wasn't satisfied.

"No. *You*—do you forgive *me*?"

"Oh yes, Dad. I forgive you. I do forgive you," I said choking back tears of my own.

"But what about mother? Does she forgive me too?"

"Oh yes, Dad. I'm sure she forgives you too."

We stood in the hall for many moments with him holding the railing and me holding him. He continued to cry, and while I couldn't read his thoughts I could see he was mentally processing something terribly important to him and I was privy to only a little. He finally looked back at me and said, "And what about God? Does he forgive me too?"

My father wasn't a man who spoke of God often but he had a deep and real Catholic faith. I didn't want to speak for God so I said, "Dad, have you asked God to forgive you?"

He nodded his balding head. "Yes. Yes, I have," he said and he became quiet. His tears dried and we started our walk again. Within ten minutes, we were back to talking about silly things like the color of the carpet and whether he had paid for dinner the previous night. But in those few moments of his asking for forgiveness, I saw deep into my father's spirit, and I learned how important forgiveness is to men, to fathers, even to heroes, because my father had always been a hero to me.

No matter who you are or what your life is like, you need to know forgiveness. It is critical to happiness and to every one of your relationships—especially with your children. Learn the art of forgiveness. Use it. Ask for it from others and give it to yourself. My father's asking me for forgiveness, for what he thought were his failures as a dad, as a husband, and as a man, made me love him even more than I already did. That moment was an enormous, precious gift for both of us.

Forgiveness and Engagement

If I could pinpoint the one thing that most often prevents fathers from having a good relationship with their kids it would be fear: fear of being rejected; fear of not being worthy; fear of conflict; fear, in the end, of asking for or giving forgiveness. But heroes never give in to fear, and neither should you.

Remember this, good men: every daughter wants her father to be closer to her. This happens in one of two ways. She either needs more time with you, or she wants to forgive you, or be forgiven by you, and heal. You just need to help her. You need to be the hero with the big helping hand who takes the lead in doing what is right.

And sons are no different. In fact, estrangement from a father can be the deepest hurt a son can feel. Boys need fathers. And just like daughters, sons need a better relationship with their dads, and if they don't have a good relationship, they will go to their graves aching for one.

So here we are back to you, the dad. You are the one who is expected to engage. Your son waits for you to move closer, to be the first to talk, ask questions, or change. You are the tough one, the strong one, the one who leads by example. Regardless of where you are in your life, you must engage first.

And, again, while it might seem daunting, it's really not that hard, and the rewards of connecting, or reconnecting, with your kids are tremendous. Good dads make it easy. Engaging kids can be simple, fun, and very straightforward. It can be as basic as doing errands together on Saturday mornings. You're not required to be an entertainer—you're just required to be there. Don't know what to talk about with your daughter? Don't worry, ask her questions about her friends, her school, or what colors she'd paint the walls in her bedroom if they all had to be a different color. Anything works.

Sons are often less verbal, which might even make it easier for you. No need to talk—just *do* things together (fishing), go places together (a hockey game), work together (making a new dining room table), or share a hobby (putting together model airplanes). Just put the phone and other electronic devices away *and engage.*

Many fathers fail to engage with their kids because they think they're not wanted. *Don't believe this*! It's true that kids don't want to be yelled at, humiliated, or criticized, and some fathers could do a better job of controlling their tempers, but every child wants to have a fun, good time with her father, or even just a happy, calm, quiet time together (like saying prayers before bed).

When Virginia was three years old, her parents divorced. She lived with her mother on Long Island during the week and she and her sisters spent every other weekend with her father, who lived not far away. She loved those weekends, and particularly remembered playing outside with her father.

Virginia's mother remarried and life changed drastically. Her stepfather had no children of his own, but he quickly established himself as an unaffectionate, rigid disciplinarian of the wrong sort—the sort who is intent on affirming his own authority and ego and in running down, rather than helping, his children. The atmosphere was so unhappy that one of Virginia's older sisters eventually went to live with her father during her college years.

"Living with my stepfather ruined my self-esteem," Virginia told me. "I could never do anything right and when I tried, it made no difference. He criticized me relentlessly."

I asked Virginia how her mother responded when her stepfather was mean to her and her siblings. "She tried to stand up for us, but she also wanted to be supportive of my stepfather. She was either going to be at odds with us or with him and she wanted to keep her marriage intact."

The girls continued to visit their father every other weekend. It was a welcome reprieve from the tension in their home. "But all of that changed when I was eleven," Virginia told me. "When I was eleven, my father decided to take a trip to see his parents in West Virginia. He wanted all of us daughters to go. One of my older sisters was unable to go and my other older sister did not want to go. I wanted to go but I was afraid that if I did, I would disappoint my mother. So I told my dad that I wasn't going. He was extremely upset. He left on the trip without me."

I had to prod Virginia for the rest of the story. "Did he call you *during* the trip? Did he talk to you *after* the trip?"

"No and no."

"You mean, you stopped seeing your father because you wouldn't go on a trip when you were eleven?"

"Yup."

Virginia's story didn't make sense, but she told me that for the next thirteen years, she never saw or spoke to her father, a man who had always been supportive and loving of her. And she needed him. Life at home with her stepfather was almost unbearable at times and Virginia lost more than just her dad and his affection when they stopped communicating. She lost hope of regaining her self-confidence.

For thirteen years, Virginia lived without any contact from her father: no letters, phone calls, or birthday cards. She found out many years later that her father had sent her a book for her thirteenth birthday, but due to her stepfather's negative influence, the books were returned to her father.

Then something extraordinary happened to Virginia. Her father left her a message via Facebook. "I didn't know what to think," she said. "I was twenty-four years old, living in another state, and I had a whole new life. I was excited, sad, and nervous, but overall happy that he reached out to me.

"I responded to my father's Facebook message and we began communicating again. But then, two days later, I was hiking with friends and had a seizure—out of the blue. I went to the doctor and he found that I had a brain tumor. Since it was quite serious, they decided to arrange surgery about a month or so after I found out I had a tumor. My dad got on a plane when he heard I was sick and came right away. He was with me right before, during, and after my surgery," she said.

"My mother came too and we were all together. It was weird but wonderful at the same time. I remember riding in the car with two of my sisters, my mother and my father together, and I was sad thinking that this is how everything could have been."

Virginia recovered from her brain tumor and kept in close touch with her father. "We are still close," she told me.

I asked her the million-dollar question. "So why did your father not contact you for thirteen years? Did you ask him?"

"No, I didn't ask him directly but I think I know what happened. When I was eleven and told him that I didn't want to go on vacation with him, he felt rejected. He believed that I didn't want him. He decided that if I didn't want him, he might as well check out. If only he understood how much I needed him. My self-esteem would have been so much better. I needed him to help me with life. Every daughter needs her father. It's hard to pinpoint specifically what I wanted and needed, but I needed him. I know that."

After her surgery, Virginia and her father spent more time together, and her father said he was sorry. He was sorry for not being there for her when she was a teen and sorry for the misunderstanding. They healed their relationship. When Virginia got married, her father walked her down the aisle.

"What you need to know," she told me, "is how healing it was to have him back, to hear him say he was sorry, and to reconnect. I can honestly say that I am a stronger person now because I have my dad back."

Thirteen years of estrangement, thirteen years of emptiness, loneliness, and loss all because of a misunderstanding—and yet, when Virginia's father re-engaged, *even when his daughter was a grown woman*, it dramatically changed her life for the better. His saying he was sorry wiped out years of pain for Virginia and helped restore her sense of self. Today, she speaks of her reconciliation with her father, and the timing of it, as a miracle given to her from God.

In my experience, many fathers are like Virginia's father. For all their strength, men are vulnerable to rejection. You hug your twelve-year-old and she pushes you away and you withdraw from the relationship. You ask your eight-year-old son to go to a hockey game and when he says he wants to stay home with his mother instead, you drop the idea of going to sporting events with your son. You ask your fifteen-year-old daughter to go to a movie and she gives you a look like you are the most disgusting person she's ever seen, so you decide she's grown beyond needing you.

There are many things that children do that break a father's heart. Whether you are a great father, an estranged one, or a father who only sees his kids several times a year, you will have many moments when you will believe in the bottom of your heart that your son or daughter really doesn't want you. As one who has listened to thousands of kids, let me tell you: the rejection you feel from them isn't rejection of you because *it isn't about you.* It's all about them and their own feelings of awkwardness or inadequacy. The important lesson to learn from Virginia and her father is this: *never allow a feeling of rejection to keep you from moving forward and engaging with your son or daughter.*

Like every hero meeting an obstacle, you need to take a deep breath and then press on because your son or daughter needs you more than they can say. Your tenacity and perseverance have to kick in, your willingness to forgive and even to apologize have to be there.

You might not feel like a hero today. I hear from fathers all the time who say, "Well, I know I'm not doing a very good job, but…"

I always ask them this question: "Why do you think you aren't doing a very good job?"

Sometimes they say they aren't patient, attentive, affectionate, or that they don't listen well enough. Whatever the reasons, *they don't matter.* They don't matter as much as your willingness to try. You don't have to be super affectionate to be a hero. You don't have to attend every soccer game or always be a good listener. Of course you have faults, all fathers do, *all heroes do.* Your faults do not preclude you from being a hero in your children's eyes.

The past is the past. What matters is what you do from now on. Your son wants more of you. Your daughter wants a few simple things from you. And when you deliver these few things, you've won. Your child will want to be with you and will respond to your overtures of engagement.

Take Inventory of Your Roadblocks

Pinpoint what is keeping you from having a stronger relationship with your kids. It might be a personality conflict, or it might be that your daughter reminds you of your ex-wife, or the fact that you come home from work exhausted and irritable and easily lose your temper, or maybe you have an addiction to gambling, sex, or alcohol that you need to deal with.

Whatever it is, men are pragmatists, list-makers, problem-solvers, and doers. So identify the problem and correct it. Often, when I talk to fathers, that's all it takes—a willingness to face up to a problem, rather than to withdraw and try to ignore it, and then a resolution to solve it. Solving your imperfect relationships with your children is entirely within your grasp. It might take work. It might take time. But with perseverance, forgiveness, and engagement, your relationships with your children will certainly be restored. What separates great fathers from the others is their commitment to removing any and all roadblocks that keep them from having the relationship that they should have with their children. You need to make that a priority, because nothing is more important to them— or ultimately to you.

Get Personal: Persevere and Forgive

You are the dad, not the kid, and you have the power to remove the roadblocks that separate you from your children; you have the power to forgive them—and to forgive yourself for having not controlled your temper or saying hurtful things or being disengaged in the past.

So forgive any family members who have wounded you. Heroic fathers don't hold grudges. They hold on to what is good and forgive the rest. Forgiveness is not only one of the greatest gifts you can give your children, it is one of the greatest gifts you can give your spouse (and yourself).

Make a Plan

We all know that women like to talk about problems, while men prefer to fix them. When it comes to your kids, fixing things is exactly what you must do. Virginia's dad healed their relationship by reaching out to her, even after more than a decade of estrangement. Was he nervous? I'm sure. Was he afraid of more rejection—or even fury or vitriol from his daughter? Probably. But he engaged with her anyway, despite every obstacle of the past, and he won.

Your son or daughter needs you, and if you want to better connect with your child, here's a simple way to start. At the end of the day, sit on the edge of their bed and ask them how their day was. It doesn't really matter what they say or even if they just say "Fine" and roll over and fall asleep. You made the gesture, and your child will take that to heart. Keep at it, and chances are not only will your child start opening up, she'll very likely look forward to these close-of-day conversations.

If you have a lot of tension or hurt in your relationship with your child, move forward slowly and persistently. Never give up trying. Set aside special time to be alone with your child. Find out what he likes to do and do it with him. Don't pull him into *your* hobbies, but move into *his* arena and share *his* passions (as far as you can—you don't need to fake anything).

With daughters, the emphasis is less on doing than on talking—and luckily for fathers, you don't have to do a lot of talking, you just have to ask specific questions and listen. Contrary to what you might think, teen girls really do like to talk to their parents, but they often feel parents don't ask the right questions or really listen to the answers they give. I can guarantee you that if you sincerely want to hear what is on your daughter's mind, what she worries about or what she's feeling, she will talk. So rather than say, "How was your day at school," ask her something like, "I know that you've been struggling with your coach being unreasonable; how is she treating your team now?"

Find out what she's interested in (friends, athletics, clothes, music) and ask her questions around those topics. One way to get conversations going is to drive her somewhere. Take her in the car and do errands together. Being stuck alone in the car can be a great time to start discussions that might otherwise not happen.

Sons grow closer to their fathers through activity. So very often, the best way to engage with them is to play catch or go to a game. These might seem like small, insignificant activities to you, but to your son, they're life-changing.

A great reflection for you as a father is to hearken back to what you would have liked your dad to have done when you were five or ten or fifteen or twenty. You have that chance now, so take advantage of it. The boy in you—and there's still a boy in every man—will like it as much as your son does.

Being a hero to your kids is simple. It isn't easy, but it is simple. Live with courage. Take the heat and bear the burdens that come with leadership. Persevere. Don't walk out. Be tenacious in love.

Speak kindly and wisely. Use your own father's example—good or bad—as a guide of things to do or to avoid. Being a hero-dad doesn't mean getting everything right; it means getting the big things right. And a lot of that comes down to effort and commitment. If you've read this book, you have the commitment, and I hope I've given you some useful pointers and tools. It's up to you to make the most of them. The game is on, and you, the hero-dad, now have to get back onto the field. I'm confident that you can win.

Acknowledgments
and Thanks

I would like to express my deep appreciation to my literary agent and friend, Shannon Litton at 5by5. You have been a champion of my work for years and I thank you for your undying support. Anne Mann, you have been with me through every page of every book, lecture, and podcast and I can't express how much I appreciate your love and faithfulness to me.

My team at Regnery has been outstanding. Harry Crocker, my editor, you are the best in the business. Maria Ruhl, you have done a wonderful job as well. I thank you, Marji Ross, for your leadership at Regnery, your friendship, and belief in my work. You are an extraordinary woman. I am thankful to my friend and advocate Bob DeMoss. Without you, this book might not exist. Thanks to

Mark Bloomfield and Alyssa Cordova, and to you, Gary Terashita, for your hard work on behalf of Regnery Faith.

Two of my team members at 5by5 deserve accolades for their professionalism and outstanding help: Grant Jenkins and Rachel Pinkerton. Andrea Lucado, you have been a tremendous help with your writing skills.

Finally, I thank the great fathers who have inspired me to write this book: Dave Ramsey, Dave Tyree, Benjamin Watson, Blake Thompson, Jeremy Breland, Les Parrott, Henry Cloud, Michael Junior, and the numerous fathers taking care of the most wonderful children in my pediatric practice.

Bibliography

This is a narrative bibliography outlined for you so that you can easily find references that will be helpful for specific questions you may have. References are grouped into issues affecting fathers only, fathers with daughters, and fathers with sons or daughters.

Father Issues

Ahrons, C. "Family ties after divorce: Long-term implications for children." *Family Process* 46 (2007).

Beaton, J., M. Hallman, and A. Dienhart. "A qualitative analysis of fathers' experiences of parental time after separation and divorce." *Fathering* 5 (2007).

Bronte-Tinkew, J. et al. "Symptoms of major depression in a sample of fathers of infants: Socio-demographic correlates and links to father involvement." *Journal of Family Issues* 28 (2007).

Castillo, J., and C. Sarver. "Nonresident father' social networks: The relationship between social support and father involvement." *Journal of the International Association for Relationship Research* 19 (2012).

Davis, R. N. et al. "Fathers' depression related to positive and negative parenting behaviors with 1-year-old children." *Pediatrics* 127 (2011).

Geller, A. "Paternal incarceration and father-child contact in fragile families." *Journal of Marriage and Family* 75 (2013).

Guzzo, K. B. "New fathers' experiences with their own fathers and attitudes toward fathering." *Fathering* 9 (2011).

Hawkins, A. J. et al. "Increasing fathers' involvement in child care with a couple-focused intervention during the transition to parenthood." *Family Relations* 57 (2008).

Helbig, S. et al. "Is parenthood associated with mental health? Findings from an epidemiological community survey." *Social Psychiatry and Psychiatric Epidemiology* 41(2006).

Holmes, E.K. and A. C. Huston. "Understanding positive father-child interaction: Children's, fathers', and mothers' contributions." *Fathering* 8 (2010).

Jones, J. and W. D. Mosher. *Fathers' involvement with their children: United States, 2006-2010.* Hyattsville, MD: National Center for Health Statistics, 2013.

Kim, P. et al. "Neural plasticity in fathers of human infants." *Social Neuroscience* 9 (2014). doi: 10.1080/17470919.2014.933713.

Lerman, R. I. "Capabilities and contributions of unwed fathers." *The Future of Children* 20 (2010).

McGill, B. S. "Navigating new norms of involved fatherhood: Employment, fathering attitudes, and father involvement." *Journal of Family Issues* 35 (2014).

McLaughlin, K. and O. Muldoon. "Father identity, involvement and work–family balance: An in-depth interview study." *Journal of Community and Applied Social Psychology* 24 (2014).

Milkie, M.A. and K. E. Denny. "Changes in the cultural model of father involvement: Descriptions of benefits to fathers, children, and mothers in parents' magazine, 1926–2006." *Journal of Family Issues* 35 (2014).

National Center for Fathering. *Fathering in America*. Kansas City, KS: National Center for Fathering, 2009.

Solomon, C.R. "I feel like a rock star: Fatherhood for stay-at-home fathers." *Fathering* 12 (2014).

Stevenson, M.M. et al. "Marital problems, maternal gatekeeping attitudes, and father-child interaction." *Developmental Psychology* 50 (2014).

Taylor, P. et al. "A tale of two fathers: More are active, but more are absent." Washington, D.C.: Pew Research Center, 2011.

Troilo, J., and M. Coleman. "Full-time, part-time full-time, and part-time fathers: Father identities following divorce." *Family Relations* 61 (2012).

Father-Daughter Issues

Albert, B. *With one voice: America's adults and teens sound off about teen pregnancy.* Washington, DC: National Campaign to Prevent Teen Pregnancy, 2007.

Antecol, H. and K. Bedard. "Does single parenthood increase the probability of teenage promiscuity, substance abuse, and crime?" *Journal of Popular Economics* 20 (2007).

Burn, V. E. "Living without a strong father figure: A context for teen mothers' experience of having become sexually active." *Issues in Mental Health Nursing* 29 (2008).

Butler, A. C. "Child sexual assault: Risk factors for girls." *Child Abuse & Neglect* 37(9) (2013).

Coley, R.L., E. Votruba-Drzal, and H. S. Schindler. "Fathers' and mothers' parenting predicting and responding to adolescent sexual risk behaviors." *Child Development* 80 (2009).

Deardorff, J. et al. "Father absence, body mass index, and pubertal timing in girls: Differential effects by family income and ethnicity." *Journal of Adolescent Health* 48(5) (2011).

East, L., D. Jackson, and L. O'Brien. "'I don't want to hate him forever': Understanding daughter's experiences of father absence." *Australian Journal of Advanced Nursing* 24 (2007).

Ellis, B. J. et al. "Impact of fathers on risky sexual behavior in daughters: A genetically and environmentally controlled sibling study." *Development and Psychopathology* 24(1) (2012).

Ellis, B.J. et al. "Does father absence place daughters at special risk for early sexual activity and teenage pregnancy?" *Child Development* 74 (2003).

Guardia, A. C. L. J. A. Nelson, and I. M. Lertora. "The impact of father absence on daughter sexual development and behaviors: Implications for professional counselors." *The Family Journal* 22(3) (2014).

Ikramullah, E. et al. *Parents matter: The role of parents in teens' decisions about sex.* Washington, DC: Child Trends, 2009.

Jordahl, T. and B. J. Lohman. "A bioecological analysis of risk and protective factors associated with early sexual intercourse of young adolescents." *Children and Youth Services Review* 31(2009).

Mitchell, K. S., A. Booth, and V. King. "Adolescents with non-resident fathers: are daughters more disadvantaged than sons?" *Journal of Marriage and Family* 71 (2009).

Reese, B. M. et al. "The association between sequences of sexual initiation and the likelihood of teenage pregnancy." *The Journal of Adolescent Health* 52(2) (2013).

Sturgeon, S.W. *The relationship between family structure and adolescent sexual activity.* Washington, DC: The Heritage Foundation, (2008).

Father-Child Issues

Adamsons, K. and S. K. Johnson. "An updated and expanded meta-analysis of nonresident fathering and child well-being." *Journal of Family Psychology* 27 (2013).

Black, K.A. and E. D. Schutte. "Recollections of being loved: Implications of childhood experiences with Parents for Young

Adults' Romantic Relationships." *Journal of Family Issues* (October 1, 2006).

Bronte-Tinkew, J. et al. "Involvement among resident fathers and links to infant cognitive outcomes." *Journal of Family Issues* 29 (2008).

Bronte-Tinkew, J., K. A. Moore, and J. Carrano. "The father-child relationship, parenting styles, and adolescent risk behaviors in intact families." *Journal of Family Issues* 27 (2006).

Carlson, M. J. "Family structure, father involvement, and adolescent behavioral outcomes." *Journal of Marriage and Family* 68 (2006).

Cavanagh, S. E. and A. C. Huston. "Family instability and children's early problem behavior." *Social Forces* 85 (2006).

Coley, R. L. and B. L. Medeiros. "Reciprocal longitudinal relations between nonresident father involvement and adolescent delinquency." *Child Development* 78 (2007).

Garfield, C. F. and A. Isacco. "Fathers and the well-child visit." *Pediatrics* 117 (2006).

Goldscheider, F. et al. "Fatherhood across two generations: Factors affecting early family roles." *Journal of Family Issues* 30 (2009).

Goncya, E.A. and M. H. van Dulmen. "Fathers do make a difference: Parental involvement and adolescent alcohol use." *Fathering* 8 (2010).

Green, B. et al. "Father involvement, dating violence, and sexual risk behaviors among a national sample of adolescent females." *Journal of Interpersonal Violence* (2014), http://jiv.sagepub.com/.

Hendricks, C. S. et al. "The influence of father absence on the self-esteem and self-reported sexual activity of rural southern adolescents." *ABNF Journal*, 16 (2005).

Keizer, R. et al. "A prospective study on father involvement and toddlers' behavioral and emotional problems: Are sons and daughters differentially affected?" *Fathering* 12 (2014).

King, V. and J. M. Sobolewski. "Nonresident fathers' contributions to adolescent well-being." *Journal of Marriage and Family* 68 (2006).

Kotila, L. and C. Dush. "Involvement with children and low-income fathers' psychological well-being." *Fathering* 11 (2013).

Kruger, D. J. et al. "Local scarcity of adult men predicts youth assault rates." *Journal of Community Psychology* 42(1) (2014).

Lewin, A. et al. "The protective effects of father involvement for infants of teen mothers with depressive symptoms." *Maternal and Child Health Journal* 19 (2015).

Lundberg, S., S. McLanahan, and E. Rose. "Child gender and father involvement in fragile families." *Demography* 44 (2007).

Martin, A., M. R. Ryan, and J. Brooks-Gunn. "When fathers' supportiveness matters most: Maternal and paternal parenting and children's school readiness." *Journal of Family Psychology* 24 (2010).

Newland, L., H. Chen, and D. Coyl-Shepherd. "Associations among father beliefs, perceptions, life context, involvement, child attachment and school outcomes in the U.S. and Taiwan." *Fathering* 11 (2013).

Nock, S. L. and C. J. Einolf. *The One Hundred Billion Dollar Man: The Annual Public Costs of Father Absence*. Germantown, MD: National Fatherhood Initiative, 2008.

Patock-Peckham, J. A. and A. A. Morgan-Lopez. "College drinking behaviors: mediational links between parenting styles, parental bonds, depression, and alcohol problems." *Psychology of Addictive Behaviors* 21 (2007).

Potter, D. "Psychological well-being and the relationship between divorce and children's academic achievement." *Journal of Marriage and Family* 72 (2010).

Pougnet, E. et al. "The intergenerational continuity of fathers' absence in a socioeconomically disadvantaged sample." *Journal of Marriage and Family* 74(3) (2012).

Reeb, B. T. and K. J. Conger. "The unique effect of paternal depressive symptoms on adolescent functioning: Associations with gender and father–adolescent relationship closeness." *Journal of Family Psychology* 23 (2010).

Saffer, B. Y., C. R. Glenn, and E. David Klonsky. "Clarifying the Relationship of Parental Bonding to Suicide Ideation and Attempts." *Suicide and Life-Threat Behavior* (2004). doi: 10.1111/sltb.12146.

Saracho, O. N. "Fathers and young children's literacy experiences in a family environment." *Early Child Development and Care* 177 (2007).

Sarkadi, A. et al. "Fathers' involvement and children's developmental outcomes: a systematic review of longitudinal studies." *Acta Pædiatrica* 97 (2008).

Schutte, E. and K. Black, "Recollections of Being Loved: Implications of Childhood Experiences with Parents for Young Adults' Romantic Relationships." *Journal of Family Issues* 27 no. 10 (2006).

General Issues

Abraham, E. et al. "Father's brain is sensitive to childcare experiences." *Proceedings of the National Academy of Sciences of the United States of America* 111 (2014).

Administration for Children and Families. *Responsible Fatherhood*. 2014. Retrieved from: http://www.acf.hhs.gov/programs/ofa/programs/healthy-marriage/responsible-fatherhood.

Alexandre, G.C. et al. "The presence of a stepfather and child physical abuse, as reported by a sample of Brazilian mothers in Rio de Janeiro." *Child Abuse & Neglect* 34 (2010).

Allen Jackson, R., R. Forste, and J. P. Bartkowski. "'Just be there for them': Perceptions of fathering among single, low income men." *Fathering* 7 (2009).

Allen, A. N. and C. C. Lo. "Drugs, guns, and disadvantaged youths: Co-occurring behavior and the code of the street." *Crime & Delinquency* 58(6) (2012).

Anthes, Emily. "Family Guy: Fathers No Longer Just Backup Parents." *Scientific American Mind* (May/June 2010).

Aquilino, W. S. "The noncustodial father-child relationship from adolescence into young adulthood."*Journal of Marriage and Family* 68 (2006).

Aria, A. M. et al. "Suicide ideation among college students: A multivariate analysis." *Archives of Suicide Research* 13 (2009).

Barnett, R. C. and K. C. Gareis. "Shift work, parenting behaviors, and children's socioemotional well-being: A within-family study." *Journal of Family Issues* 28 (2007).

Bendheim-Thomas Center for Research on Child Wellbeing and Social Indicators Survey Center. "CPS involvement in families with social fathers." *Fragile Families Research Brief* (2006).

Bendheim-Thomas Center for Research on Child Wellbeing and Social Indicators Survey Center. "CPS involvement in families with social fathers." *Fragile Families Research Brief* (2010).

———. "Predictors of homelessness and doubling-up among at-risk families." *Fragile Families Research Brief* 43 (2008).

———. "Parents' relationship status five years after a non-marital birth." *Fragile Families Research Brief* 39 (2007).

Berger, L. M., M. Cancian, and D. R. Meyer. "Maternal re-partnering and new-partner fertility: Associations with nonresident father investments in children." *Children and Youth Services Review* 34 (2012).

Bryan, D. M. "To parent or provide? The effect of the provider role on low-income men's decisions about fatherhood and paternal engagement." *Fathering* 11 (2013).

Butler, A. C. "Child sexual assault: Risk factors for girls." *Child Abuse & Neglect* 37(9) (2013).

Bzostek, S. H., M. J. Carlson, and S. S. McLanahan. *Mother's union formation following a nonmarital birth: Does mother know best?* Working paper #2006-27-FF. Princeton, NJ: Center for Research on Child Wellbeing, Princeton University, 2007.

Cancian, M. et al. "Who gets custody now? Dramatic changes in children's living arrangements after divorce." *Demography* 51 (2014).

Carlson, M. J. and F. F. Furstenberg. "The prevalence and correlates of multipartnered fertility among urban U.S. parents." *Journal of Marriage and Family* 68 (2006).

Castillo, J. G. Welch, and C. Sarver. "Walking a high beam: The balance between employment stability, workplace flexibility, and nonresident father involvement." *American Journal of Men's Health* 6 (2012).

Cavanagh, K., R. E. Dobash, and R. P. Dobash. "The murder of children by fathers in the context of child abuse." *Child Abuse & Neglect* 31 (2007).

Cobb-Clark, D. A. and E. Tekin. "Fathers and youths' delinquent behavior." *Review of Economics of the Household* 12(2) (2014).

Coley, R. L. and B. L. Medeiros, B. L. "Reciprocal longitudinal relations between nonresident father involvement and adolescent delinquency." *Child Development* 78 (2007).

Creech, S.K., W. Hadley, W., and B. Bosari. "The impact of military deployment and reintegration on children and parenting: A systematic review." *Professional Psychology: Research and Practice* 45 (2014).

Fabricius, W, V. and L. J. Luecken. "Post divorce living arrangements parent conflict, and long-term physical health correlates for children of divorce." *Journal of Family Psychology* 21.

Fomby, P. and A. J. Cherlin. "Family instability and child well-being." *American Sociological Review* 72 (2007).

Freeman, H. and T. M. Almond. "Mapping young adults' use of fathers for attachment support: implications on romantic relationship experiences." *Early Child Development & Care* 180 (2012).

Galovan, A. et al. "Father involvement, father-child relationship quality, and satisfaction with family work: Actor and partner influences on marital quality." *Journal of Family Issues* 35 (2014).

Geller, A. et al. "Beyond Absenteeism: Father incarceration and child development." *Demography* 49 (2011).

Gibson-Davis, C. M. "Family structure effects on maternal and paternal parenting in low-income families." *Journal of Marriage and Family* 70 (2008).

Glenn, N. and B. D. Whitehead. *Mama Says: A National Survey of Mothers' Attitudes on Fathering.* Germantown, MD: National Fatherhood Initiative, 2009.

Glenn, N. and D. Popenoe, D. *Pop's Culture: A National Survey of Dads' Attitudes on Fathering.* Germantown, MD: National Fatherhood Initiative, 2006.

Goldberg, J. S. "Identity and involvement among resident and nonresident fathers." *Journal of Family Issues* 36 (2015).

Grall, Timothy. *Custodial Mothers and Fathers and Their Child Support: 2007.* Washington, DC: U.S. Census Bureau, 2009.

———. *Custodial Mothers and Fathers and Their Child Support: 2011.* Washington, DC: U.S. Census Bureau, 2013.

Guterman, N.B. et al. "Fathers and maternal risk for physical child abuse." *Child Maltreatment* 14 (2009).

Harcourt, K. T. et al. "Examining family structure and half-sibling influence on adolescent well-being." *Journal of Family Issues* 36(2) (2015).

Hilton, N. Z., G. T. Harris and M. E. Rice. "The step-father effect in child abuse: Comparing discriminative parental solicitude and antisociality." *Psychology of Violence* 5(1) (2015).

Hofferth, S. L. "Residential father family type and child well-being: investment versus selection." *Demography* 43 (2006).

Hognas, R. S. and M. J. Carlson. "Like parent, like child?: The intergenerational transmission of nonmarital childbearing." *Social Science Research* 41 (2012).

Jablonska, B. and L. Lindberg. "Risk behaviours, victimisation and mental distress among adolescents in different family structures." *Social Psychiatry & Psychiatric Epidemiology* 42 (2007).

Jethwani, M. R. Mincy, and S. Klempin. "I would like them to get where I never got to: Nonresident fathers' presence in the educational lives of their children." *Children and Youth Services Review* 40 (2014).

Kalmijn, M. "Long-term effects of divorce on parent-child relationships: Within-family comparisons of fathers and mothers." *European Sociological Review* 29 (2013).

Kane, J. B., T. J. Nelson, and K. Edin. "How much in-kind support do low-income nonresident fathers provide? A mixed-method analysis." *Journal of Marriage and Family* (2015) doi/10.1111/jomf.12188/references.

King, V. "When children have two mothers: relationships with nonresident mothers, stepmothers, and fathers." *Journal of Marriage and Family* 69 (2007).

Knoester, C. and D. A. Hayne. "Community context, social integration into family, and youth violence." *Journal of Marriage and Family* 67 (2005).

Kreider, R. M. "Living arrangements of children: (2004)." *Current Population Reports* P70–114. Washington, DC: U.S. Census Bureau, 2008.

Lang, D. L. et al. "Multi-level factors associated with pregnancy among urban adolescent women seeking psychological services." *Journal of Urban Health* 90 (2013).

Lee, C. S. and W. J. Doherty. "Marital satisfaction and father involvement during the transition to parenthood." *Fathering* 5 (2007).

Li, K., et al. "Drinking and parenting practices are predictors of impaired driving behaviors among U.S. adolescents." *Journal of Studies on Alcohol and Drugs* 75(1) (2014).

Luscombe, B. "Marriage: What's it Good For?" *Time* 176 (2015).

Manlove, J. et al. "Family environments and the relationship context of first adolescent sex: Correlates of first sex in a casual versus steady relationship."*Social Science Research* 41(4) (2012).

Manning, W. D. et al. "Cohabitation expectation among young adults in the United States: Do they match behavior?" *Population Research and Policy Review* 33 (2014).

Martin, J. et al. "Births: Final data for 2012." *National Vital Statistics Reports* 62(9). Hyattsville, MD: National Center for Health Statistics, 2013.

Martin, S. P. "Trends in marital dissolution by women's education in the United States." *Demographic Research* 15 (2006).

McClain, L. and A. DeMaris. "A better deal for cohabitating fathers? Union status differences in father involvement." *Fathering* 11 (2013).

McLanahan, S. "Fragile families and the reproduction of poverty." *Annals of the American Academy of Political and Social Science* 621 (2009).

Mehall, K.G. et al. "Examining the relations of infant temperament and couples' marital satisfaction to mother and father involvement: A longitudinal study." *Fathering* 7 (2009).

Mokrue, K., Y. Y. Chen, and M. Elias. "The interaction between family structure and child gender on behavior problems in urban ethnic minority children." *International Journal of Behavioral Development* 36(2) (2011; 2012).

Murray, J., D. P. Farrington, and I. Sekol. "Children's antisocial behavior, mental health, drug use, and educational performance after parental incarceration: A systematic review and meta-analysis." *Psychological Bulletin American Psychological Association* 138 (2012).

Nepomnyaschy, L. "Fathers' involvement with their nonresident children and material hardship." *Social Service Review* 85 (2011).

Oldehikinel, A. J. et al. "Parental divorce and offspring depressive symptoms: Dutch developmental trends during early adolescence." *Journal of Marriage and Family* 70 2008.

Osborne, C. and S. McLanahan. "Partnership instability and child well-being." *Journal of Marriage and Family* 69 2007.

Palmer, E. J. and K. Gough. "Childhood experiences of parenting and causal attributions for criminal behavior among young offenders and non-offenders." *Journal of Applied Social Psychology* 37 (2007).

Patock-Peckham, J. A. and A. A. Morgan-Lopez. "College drinking behaviors: Mediational links between parenting styles, parental bonds, depression, and alcohol problems." *Psychology of Addictive Behaviors* 21(3) 2007.

Paulson, J. F., H. A. Keefe, and J. A. Leiferman. "Early parental depression and child language development." *Journal of Child Psychology and Psychiatry* 50 (2009).

Puhlman, D. and K. Pasley. "Rethinking maternal gatekeeping." *Journal of Family Theory & Review* 5 (2013).

Ramchandani, P. G. et al. "Do early father–infant interactions predict the onset of externalising behaviours in young children? Findings from a longitudinal cohort study." *Journal of Child Psychology and Psychiatry* 54 (2013).

Raub, J. C. et al. "Predictors of custody and visitation decisions by a family court clinic." *Journal of the American Academy of Psychiatry and the Law Online* 41 (2013).

Reed, S., J. Bell, and T. Edwards. "Adolescent well-being in Washington State military families." *American Journal of Public Health* 101 (2011).

Ryan, R. M. "Nonresident fatherhood and adolescent sexual behavior: A comparison of siblings approach." *Developmental Psychology* 51(2) (2015).

Sawhill, I. V. "Teenage sex, pregnancy, and nonmarital births." *Gender Issues* 23 (2006).

Schmeer, K. K. "The child health disadvantage of parental cohabitation." *Journal of Marriage and Family* 73(1) (2011).

Schoen, R., N. S. Lansdale, and K. Daniels. "Family transitions in young adulthood." *Demography* 44.

Shah, M., R. Gee, and K. Theall. "Partner support and impact on birth outcomes among teen pregnancies in the United States." *Journal of Pediatric and Adolescent Gynecology* 27 (2014).

Smaldone, A., J. C. Honig, and M. W. Byrne. "Sleepless in America: inadequate sleep and relationships to health and wellbeing of our nation's children." *Pediatrics* 119 (2007).

Smith Stover, C. and A. Spink. "Affective awareness in parenting of fathers with co-occurring substance abuse and intimate partner violence." *Advances in Dual Diagnosis* 5 (2013).

Smith Stover, C., C. Easton, and T. J. McMahon. "Parenting of men with co-occurring intimate partner violence and substance abuse." *Journal of Interpersonal Violence* 28 (2015).

Sobolewski, J. M. and P. R. Amato. "Parents' discord and divorce, parent-child relationships and subjective well-being in early adulthood: is feeling close to two parents always better than feeling close to one?" *Social Forces* 85 (2007).

Stykes, J. *Nonresident Father Visitation (FP-12-02)*. Bowling Green, OH: National Center for Family & Marriage Research, Bowling Green State University, 2012.

Taylor, P. et al. "A tale of two fathers: More are active, but more are absent."

Tillman, K. H. "Family structure pathways and academic disadvantage among adolescents in stepfamilies." *Journal of Marriage and Family* 77 (2007).

Turner, H. A. et al. "Family structure, victimization, and child mental health in a nationally representative sample." *Social Science & Medicine* 87 (2013).

Turneya, K. and C. Wildeman, C. "Redefining relationships: Explaining the countervailing consequences of paternal incarceration for parenting." *American Sociological Review* 78 (2013).

U.S. Census Bureau. "Children/1 by presence and type of parent(s), race, and hispanic origin/2: 2014. Table C9." Washington, DC: U.S. Census Bureau, 2015.

U.S. Census Bureau. "Living arrangements of children under 18 years/1 and marital status of parents, by age, sex, race, and Hispanic origin/2 and selected characteristics of the child for all children: 2014." Washington, DC: U.S. Census Bureau, 2015.

U.S. Census Bureau. *America's families and living arrangements: 2012.* Washington, DC: U.S. Census Bureau, 2013.

———. *Facts for Features: Father's Day: June 15, 2014.* Washington, DC: U.S. Census Bureau.

———. *Live births, deaths, marriages, and divorces: 1960 to 2008.* Washington, DC: U.S. Census Bureau, 2012.

U.S. Department of Health and Human Services. *Information on poverty and income statistics: A summary of 2012 current population survey data.* 2012. Retrieved from: http://aspe.hhs.gov/hsp/12/PovertyAndIncomeEst/ib.cfm.

U.S. Department of Health and Human Services, Administration for Children and Families, Administration on Children, Youth and Families, Children's Bureau. *Child Maltreatment 2013*. Retrieved from http://www.acf.hhs.gov/sites/default/ files/cb/cm2013.pdf.

Vaszari, J. M. et al. "Risk factors for suicidal ideation in a population of community-recruited female cocaine users." *Comprehensive Psychiatry* 52 (2011).

Wake, M. et al. "Preschooler obesity and parenting styles of mothers and fathers: Australian national population study." *Pediatrics* 12 (2007).

Waller, M. "Cooperation, conflict or disengagement? Coparenting styles and father involvement in fragile families." *Family Process* 51 (2012).

Waller, M. R. and A. Dwyer Emory. "Parents apart: Differences between unmarried and divorcing parents in separated families." *Family Court Review* 52 (2014).

Western, B. and B. Pettit. "Collateral costs: incarceration's effect on economic mobility." Washington, DC: The Pew Charitable Trusts, 2010.

Wright, C. L. and M. J. Levitt. "Parental absence, academic competence, and expectations in Latino immigrant youth." *Journal of Family Issues* 35(13) (2014).

Zhang, S. and T. Fuller. "Neighborhood disorder and paternal involvement of nonresident and resident fathers." *Family Relations* 61(3) (2012).

Ziol-Guest, K. M. and R. E. Dunifon. "Complex Living Arrangements and Child Health: Examining Family Structure Linkages with Children's Health Outcomes." *Family Relations* 63 (2014).

Zito, R. C. "Family structure history and teenage cohabitation: Instability, socioeconomic disadvantage, or transmission?" *Journal of Family Issues* 36(3) 2015.

Below are resources that I handpicked for fathers who want more support.

Father Resources

1. *National Fatherhood Initiative*: http://www.fatherhood.org/. This organization has wonderful resources for fathers in all different situations.

2. *National Center for Fathering*: http://www.fathers.com/.

3. *National Responsible Fatherhood Clearinghouse*: https://www.fatherhood.gov/toolkit/home.

4. *International Center of Fatherhood*: http://icfatherhood.org/about-us/.

5. *Ken Canfield, Ph.D.*: http://www.kencanfield.com/.

6. *Every Man Ministries, Dr. Ken Canfield*: https://www.every-manministries.com.

7. *Fatherhood Research and Practice Network*: www.frpn.org.

Books

1. Meg Meeker, *Strong Fathers, Strong Daughters: Ten Secrets Every Father Should Know* (Washington, DC: Regnery Publishing, 2007). I wrote *Strong Fathers, Strong Daughters* to

show fathers who they are through their daughters' eyes. It is inspirational and continues to be a bestseller after many years.

2. Ken Canfield, *Seven Secrets of Effective Fathers* (Carol Stream, IL: Tyndale Publishing, 1992). Dr. Ken Canfield is a father expert. He has been involved with helping fathers for many years and knows the research available, but also understands the "how-tos" in helping fathers. This book is practical and easy to understand. I recommend this for any struggling father.

3. Gary Smalley and John Trent, *The Blessing* (Nashville: Thomas Nelson, 2004). This is a book for fathers who never experienced the "blessing" by their own fathers. It is excellent, from men who had a tumultuous relationship with their fathers. Fathers repeat cycles of pain they experienced with their fathers onto their sons. This is a book for every father who wants to break that cycle. It also has a workbook.

4. A. W. Tozer, *The Attributes of God: The Journey into a Father's Heart* (Christian Publications, 1996). This is outstanding reading for men who want to understand God the Father better. No one is more brilliant at describing this than theologian A. W. Tozer.

5. Paul Raeburn, *Do Fathers Matter? What Science is Telling Us About the Parent We've Overlooked* (New York: Scientific American, 2014). This is an excellent book that outlines more excellent research about fathers. The data in the book is scientifically sound and clearly shows the overwhelming importance of fathers in their children's eyes. If nothing else, go to a library or bookstore and flip through the chapters. By scanning the book for ten minutes, you will see the abundance of research supporting the importance of a father's influence.

6. Ken Canfield, *The Heart of a Father: How You Can Become a Dad of Destiny* (Chicago: Northfield Press, 1996). This is an older book but the content is evergreen. If you like Dr. Canfield's philosophy and are a father interested in making an impact on your own children as well as grandchildren, this is an excellent resource

Notes

Chapter 1: You Are a Hero

1. Emily Anthes, "Family Guy: Fathers No Longer Just Backup Parents," *Scientific American Mind* (May/June 2010), https://www.scientificamerican.com/article/family-guy/.
2. Ibid.
3. A. Sarkadi et al., "Fathers' involvement and children's developmental outcomes: a systematic review of longitudinal studies," *Acta Pædiatrica* 97 (2008): 153–158.
4. Ibid.
5. *The FII-ONews*, Newsletter of the Father Involvement Initiative—Ontario Network vol. 1 (Fall 2002), http://www.ecdip.org/docs/pdf/IF%20Father%20Res%20Summary%20(KD).pdf.

6. Amato, 1994; Barber & Thomas, 1986; Barnett, Marshall, & Pleck, 1992; Bell, 1969; Furstenberg & Harris, 1993; Harris, Furstenberg, & Marmer, 1998; Lozoff, 1974; Snarey, 1993.
7. Kyle Pruett, *Fatherneed: Why Father Care is as Essential as Mother Care for Your Child* (New York, NY: Harmony, 2001).

Chapter 5: Three Questions Your Child Needs You to Answer

1. E.A. Goncya, and M. H. van Dulmena, "Fathers do make a difference: Parental involvement and adolescent alcohol use," *Fathering* 8 (2010): 93–108.
2. Julie Louise Gerberding, M.D., M.P.H. *Report to Congress: Prevention of Genital Human Papillomavirus Infection*, Centers for Disease Control and Prevention, Department of Health and Human Services Director, January 2004, https://www.cdc.gov/std/hpv/2004hpv-report.pdf.
3. Thomas J. Fitch, "How Effective Are Condoms in Preventing Pregnancy and STDs in Adolescents?" Austin, Tex: The Medical Institute, July 1997.

Index

Hear From Dr. Meg Daily!

Be sure to check out Dr. Meg's blog where she answers parents' questions and covers topics surrounding technology, family dynamics, stress, relationships and more!

FOLLOW HER ONLINE

 facebook.com/megmeekermd

 @MegMeekerMD

 @MegMeekerMD

MegMeekerMD.com/Blog